Leader: It is the Lord who blesses the work of our hands. Let us bring to his altar the tokens of our thankfulness in our offering for this day.

Congregation: Our offerings symbolize that all we have and all we are come from God. With thanks we return a part of what is His to Him as an act of thanksgiving.

Let the word of Christ dwell in you richly as you teach and admonish one another in all wisdom and as you sing psalms and hymns and spiritual songs with thankfulness in your heart to God.
Colossians 3:16

SAINT LOUIS

CONTENTS

FOREWORD

All God's People Sing! is a collection of liturgies and songs to help people pray, praise, and give thanks. Although the contents have been selected especially with God's people ages 9–14 in mind, it is believed that this book will appeal to persons of all ages. This songbook can be used in almost any setting in which Christians gather. We hope this book will be found in parochial schools, churches, homes, and camps.

Many different kinds of music are included. There are chorales, chants, folk hymns, Gospel hymns, spirituals, Taizé refrains, and selections from contemporary Christian musicians. This variety reflects the richness of the Church's treasury of song.

Several different, simple, straight-forward liturgies are provided. Some find as their theme the seasons of the church year. Others are of a more general focus. Luther's Small Catechism, the Apostles' Creed, and many prayers are also offered to enhance this book's usefulness.

The editorial committee for *All God's People Sing!* included Arnold Schmidt from the Board for Parish Services of The Lutheran Church—Missouri Synod, James Brauer of the LCMS Commission on Worship, and Barry L. Bobb representing Concordia Publishing House. This committee wishes to thank the hundreds of Sunday school teachers, day school teachers, musicians, and pastors who responded over an 18-month period to a call for song suggestions. Appreciation is also expressed to the song selection committee—Becky Rohm, Mary Feldt, Gwen Hohle, and Allen Loesel as well as to Carlos Puig and Rachel Orlando and Frazier Odom for their suggestions from the Spanish and African-American hymnal committees respectively. Thanks to Paul Prange, David Christian, and Gerald P. Coleman who were responsible for creating the liturgies as well as to the LCMS Commission on Worship members, William Otte and Gregory Wismar, for their careful review of the materials and thoughtful suggestions.

All God's People Sing! is presented to the church with the prayer that it will find great usefulness in parish life.

"All God's People Sing" because . . .

of who God is:

The One who has created us and who still provides for us in every way

The One who has redeemed us from sin, death, and the power of the devil

The One who calls, gathers, and blesses us with every spiritual gift

of who we are:

God's own people through Baptism, members of His family—the Church

- Using our everyday, plain speaking voice is *not* enough in expressing our praise and thanks to One so great.

- God's people have always been a singing people from Old Testament times to the present.

- Singing remains a key part of our celebrating, our remembering.

- Through singing we witness to others.

- Through singing we learn the Christian faith.

- God's wants us to sing—everyone, no matter how "nice" our voice is!

"Since Love is Lord of heaven and earth,
how can I keep from singing" (*Spiritual folk song*).

"Oh, come, let us sing to the Lord.
Let us make a joyful noise to Him with songs of praise" (*Psalm 95*).

WORSHIP RESOURCES

Worship is . . .

- an encounter with God.

  Our Lord speaks—He forgives, teaches, sends His Spirit.

  We listen and respond—confessing our sin, hearing His Word, telling others the Good News, serving others in His name, praying for our own needs and the needs of others.

- an active verb. It requires something of us in mind, emotions, and all our senses.

- the central activity of the Church.

- our "right and duty" as baptized members of the body of Christ.

- how we show reverence and awe.

- how we express praise, thanks, and prayers.

- something Christians do together on earth and will join together doing in eternity.

"Let the word of Christ dwell in you richly as you teach and admonish one another with all wisdom, and as you sing psalms, hymns and spiritual songs with gratitude in your hearts to God" (*Colossians 3:15–16*).

"Worthy is the Lamb, who was slain, to receive power and wealth and wisdom and strength and honor and glory and praise!" (*Revelation 5:12*).

LITURGIES

ADVENT

Leader: Lift up your heads and open your eyes,
People: for He is coming.
Leader: Who is coming?
People: The King of glory!
Leader: Blessings on Him who comes as King,
People: who comes in the name of the Lord.

ADVENT HYMN

Leader: As we light our Advent wreath, we remember the One who comes—Jesus, the light of the world.

(Someone lights the appropriate candle[s].)

Leader: He came as a baby in a manger.
People: Come, Lord Jesus.
Leader: He came to be our Savior.
People: Come, Lord Jesus.
Leader: With joy and gladness,
People: we celebrate His coming.

Leader: He comes to us each day in the promise of His presence.
People: Come, Lord Jesus.
Leader: Let us open our hearts to Him,
People: and walk in His ways.
Leader: He will come again to take us to Himself in heaven.
People: Come, Lord Jesus.

MAGNIFICAT ("My soul proclaims")

Leader: The Lord be with you.
People: And also with you.
Leader: Let us pray.

(An Advent prayer)

8

SCRIPTURE READING

MESSAGE

OFFERING

PRAYERS (*optional*)

LORD'S PRAYER

BENEDICTION

CHRISTMAS/EPIPHANY

CANDLE PROCESSION

(A large, lighted white candle [not the paschal candle] is brought down the aisle of the church or through the worship area. The following is spoken three times during the processional, with silence between.)

Leader: The light of Christ.
People: Thanks be to God.

(After the candle is put in its place, the following verses from Psalm 27 are spoken.)

Leader: The Lord is my light and my salvation—whom shall I fear?
People: The Lord is my light and my salvation.
Leader: The Lord is the stronghold of my life—of whom shall I be afraid?
People: The Lord is my light and my salvation.
Leader: Hear my voice when I call, O Lord; be merciful to me and answer me.
People: The Lord is my light and my salvation.
Leader: Teach me Your way, O Lord.
People: The Lord is my light and my salvation.
Leader: Wait for the Lord; be strong and take heart and wait for the Lord.
People: The Lord is my light and my salvation.

Leader: The Lord be with you.
People: And also with you.
Leader: Let us pray.

(An Epiphany prayer)

GLORIA IN EXCELSIS ("Glory to God in the highest")

SCRIPTURE READING

HYMN/SONG

MESSAGE

OFFERING

PRAYERS (*optional*)

LORD'S PRAYER

CLOSING HYMN (*optional*)

BENEDICTION

Leader: The grace of our Lord Jesus Christ, the love of God, and the fellowship of the Holy Spirit be with us all.

People: Amen.

LENT

CROSS PROCESSIONAL

(The following is spoken three times during the processional, with silence between.)

> Leader: Behold, the Lamb of God!
> **People: Lord, have mercy.**

INVOCATION

> Leader: O God, Father in heaven,
> **People: have mercy on us.**
> Leader: O Son of God, Redeemer of the world,
> **People: have mercy on us.**
> Leader: O God, the Holy Spirit,
> **People: have mercy on us.**

AGNUS DEI ("Lamb of God")

PSALM 51

> Reader 1: Have mercy on me, O God, according to Your unfailing love; according to Your great compassion, blot out my transgressions.
> Leader: Lamb of God, who takes away the sin of the world,
> **People: have mercy on us.**
> Reader 2: Create in me a pure heart, O God, and renew a steadfast spirit within me.
> Leader: Lamb of God, who takes away the sin of the world,
> **People: have mercy on us.**
> Reader 3: O Lord, open my lips, and my mouth will declare Your praise.
> Leader: Lamb of God, who takes away the sin of the world,
> **People: grant us peace.**

PRAYERS

> Leader: O Lord, let Your mercy be upon us,
> **People: as our trust is in You.**
> Leader: Hear our prayer, O Lord,
> **People: and let our cry come unto You.**
> Leader: The Lord be with you.
> **People: And also with you.**
> Leader: Let us pray.

(A Lenten prayer)

AGNUS DEI ("Lamb of God") is sung a second time.

SCRIPTURE READING

HYMN/SONG

MESSAGE

OFFERING

PRAYERS *(optional)*

LORD'S PRAYER

BENEDICTION

AGNUS DEI ("Lamb of God") is sung a third time.

EASTER

(The liturgy may begin with a processional that includes a paschal candle, an Easter banner, or processional cross.)

Leader: In the name of the Father and of the ✢ Son and of the Holy Spirit.
People: Amen.
Leader: The Lord is risen!
People: He is risen indeed!
Leader: Sing to the Lord a new song,
People: for He has done marvelous things.

(Sung)

Leader: Now all the vault of heaven resounds
         In praise of love that still abounds:
People: "Christ has triumphed! He is living!"
Leader: Sing choirs of angels, loud and clear!
         Repeat their song of glory here:
People: "Christ has triumphed! Christ has triumphed!"
         Alleluia, alleluia, alleluia!

(Text © 1958 *Service Book and Hymnal*. Used by permission.)

(Spoken)

Leader: The Lord is my strength and my song;
People: He has become my salvation.
Leader: Give thanks to the Lord, for He is good;
People: His love endures forever.
Leader: This is the day the Lord has made;
People: let us rejoice and be glad in it.

(Sung)

All: **Adoring praises now we bring**
         And with the heavenly blessed sing:
         "Christ has triumphed! Alleluia!"
         Be to the Father and our Lord,
         To Spirit blest, most holy God.
         All the glory, never ending!
         Alleluia, alleluia, alleluia!

(Text © 1958 *Service Book and Hymnal*. Used by permission.)

PRAYERS

Leader: The Lord be with you.
People: And also with you.
Leader: Let us pray.

(An Easter prayer)

SONG "This Is the Feast of Victory"

SCRIPTURE READING

MESSAGE

OFFERING

PRAYERS *(optional)*

LORD'S PRAYER

BENEDICTION

CLOSING HYMN/SONG

LITURGY OF PRAISE

INVOCATION (*spoken rhythmically*)

> Leader: In the name of God the Father:
> **People: Praise to our creating God!**
> Leader: In the name of His Son, Jesus:
> **People: Praise to our redeeming God!**
> Leader: In the name of God the Spirit:
> **People: Praise to our renewing God!**
> Leader: Let us join our thankful voices,
> **People: Amen! Amen! Praise the Lord!**

HYMN OF PRAISE (*May be spoken or sung.*)

[*The tune is from "This Is a Joyous, Happy Day," p. 238.*]

> Leader: From all that dwell below the skies
> Let the creator's praise arise;
> **People: Alleluia, alleluia!**
> Leader: Let the redeemer's name be sung
> Through every land, by every tongue.
> **People: Alleluia, alleluia, alleluia, alleluia, alleluia!**
> Leader: Eternal are Your mercies, Lord;
> Eternal truth attends Your Word;
> **People: Alleluia, alleluia!**
> Leader: Your praise shall sound from shore to shore
> Till suns shall rise and set no more.
> **People: Alleluia, alleluia, alleluia, alleluia, alleluia!**

PRAYERS

(*Silence for meditation or prayer follows each petition.*)

Praise to You, O Lord, for Your daily goodness and mercy.
Renew our hearts with thankfulness to You.
Alert us to the needs of others around us.
Inspire us to worship You in spirit and in truth.
Save us from our own sins, from death, and from the devil.
Energize us for service and for witness.

> **People** (*sung or spoken*):
> **All praise to God the Father be,**
> **All praise, eternal Son, to Thee;**
> **Alleluia, alleluia!**

Whom with the Spirit we adore
Forever and forevermore:
Alleluia, alleluia, alleluia, alleluia, alleluia!

SCRIPTURE READING

PSALM OF PRAISE (Psalm 150)

Leader: Praise God!
People: Praise God!
Leader: Praise Him in His holy temple, in the firmament of His power.
People: Praise God!
Leader: Praise Him for His mighty acts and His excellent greatness.
People: Praise God!
Leader: Praise Him with the blast of the trumpet, with lyre, with harp, with timbrel and dance.
People: Praise God!
Leader: Praise Him with strings and organs and with loud, resounding cymbals.
People: Praise God!
Leader: Let everything that has breath praise Him.
People: Praise God!
Leader: Praise the Lord!
People: Alleluia!

HYMN/SONG

MESSAGE

OFFERING

PRAYERS

(*Time may be allowed for prayers and petitions from individuals or from the leader; then the prayers conclude:*)

Leader: The Lord is good and His love endures forever;
People: His faithfulness continues through all generations.

LORD'S PRAYER

BENEDICTION

CLOSING HYMN

THANKSGIVING

Leader: Oh, give thanks unto the Lord, for He is good.
People: His steadfast love endures forever.

LITANY OF THANKS

Leader: Let us thank God with our hearts.
(*A brief silence*)
We remember that it is God who has given us our life,
who renews His love to us each day.
People: We thank You, Lord.
Leader: Bless the Lord, O my soul and forget not all His benefits.
People: We thank You, Lord.
Leader: It is God who forgives our sin and remembers it no more.
People: We thank You, Lord.
Leader: It is with our hearts and hands that we receive the many gifts that
God has for us.
People: We thank You, Lord.
Leader: We thank God not only with our minds, but also with our voices.
People: We thank You, Lord.
Leader: For the gifts of body and soul, eyes, ears, and all our members, our
reason and all our senses, for all that He gives to support our bodily
life,
People: we thank You, Lord.
Leader: From everlasting to everlasting the Lord's love is with His children.
People: Alleluia! Amen!

SONG OF THANKSGIVING

SCRIPTURE READING

MESSAGE

OFFERING

(*The worshipers come forward and place their offering at the altar as a thankful
response to God's many blessings.*)

PRAYERS (*optional*)

LORD'S PRAYER

BENEDICTION

BAPTISMAL REMEMBRANCE

Leader: In the name of the Father and of the ✠ Son and of the Holy Spirit.
People: Amen.

Leader: There is one body and one Spirit.
People: There is one hope in God's call to us.
Leader: One Lord, one faith, one Baptism.
People: One God and Father of us all.
Leader: As Christ was raised up from the dead by the glory of the Father,
People: even so we also should walk in the newness of life.

EASTER OR BAPTISMAL SONG

SCRIPTURE READING (Roman 6:3-11)
(*or another appropriate reading*)

REMEMBERING OUR BAPTISM

Leader: In Holy Baptism our sins are forgiven and we are granted a new life in Christ, our Lord. We solemnly renounce the devil and all his works and all his ways; we confess the gift of faith in God the Father, the Son, and the Holy Spirit.

I ask you anew:
Do you renounce the devil and all his works and all his ways?
People: I do renounce them.

Leader: Do you believe in God, the Father Almighty?
People: Yes, I believe in God, the Father Almighty, maker of heaven and earth.

Leader: Do you believe in Jesus Christ, His only Son?
People: Yes, I believe in Jesus Christ, His only Son, our Lord,
who was conceived by the Holy Spirit,
born of the Virgin Mary,
suffered under Pontius Pilate,
was crucified, died, and was buried.
He descended into hell.
The third day He rose again from the dead.
He ascended into heaven and sits at the right hand of God
the Father Almighty.
From thence He will come to judge the living and the dead.

Leader: Do you believe in the Holy Spirit?
**People: Yes, I believe in the Holy Spirit,
the holy Christian Church,
the communion of saints,
the forgiveness of sins,
the resurrection of the body,
and the life everlasting. Amen.**

Leader: Let us pray:
Almighty God, we give thanks that Your Son Jesus suffered and died for our sins. We celebrate with joy His resurrection from the dead and ascension into heaven. We are grateful for the work of Your Holy Spirit in us, which brought us to faith by Baptism. We know that You are faithful in Your covenant with us. Keep us faithful as well. Show us the way You would have us live. In Jesus, our blessed Savior.
People: Amen.

MESSAGE

SONG (*The offering may be received.*)

PRAYERS

LORD'S PRAYER

BLESSING

Leader: The grace of our Lord Jesus Christ,
the love of God, and the communion
of the Holy Spirit be with us all.
People: Amen.

WISDOM AND KNOWLEDGE

SONG

Leader: In the name of the Father, and of the ✛ Son, and of the Holy Spirit.
People: Amen.
Leader: The fear of the Lord is the beginning of wisdom.
People: To Him belongs eternal praise.
Leader: Those who practice the fear of the Lord have good understanding.
People: To Him belongs eternal praise.
Leader: So teach us to number our days, that we may apply our hearts to wisdom.
People: To Him belongs eternal praise.
Leader: For in Christ are hid all the treasures of wisdom and knowledge.
People: To Him belongs eternal praise.
Leader: Him we proclaim, warning everyone and teaching everyone in all wisdom, that we may present everyone mature in Christ.
People: To Him belongs eternal praise.

SCRIPTURE READING

MESSAGE

SONG

OFFERING

PRAYERS

Leader: Lord, hear us as we pray:
for all schools and those who teach and those who learn:
for all the schools of the Church:
for the colleges and seminaries of the Church:
for all teachers and students of the Word:
for all missionaries and evangelists:
for our teachers:
for our students:

BENEDICTION

Leader: The grace of our Lord Jesus Christ, the love of God, and the communion of the Holy Spirit be with us all.

People: Amen.

HEALTH AND HEALING

Leader: In the name of the Father, and of the ✠ Son, and of the Holy Spirit.
People: Amen.

Leader: I will exalt You, O Lord,
People: for You lifted me out of the depths.
Leader: O Lord, my God, I called to You for help,
People: and You healed me.
Leader: O Lord, my God,
People: I will give You thanks forever.

SCRIPTURE READING

MESSAGE

SONG

OFFERING

PRAYERS

(The leader takes time to gather the prayer concerns of those present. Pray for the sick by name.)

LORD'S PRAYER

Leader: Lord, remember us in Your kingdom, and teach us to pray:
People: Our Father who art in heaven . . .

BENEDICTION

Leader: The Lord bless you and keep you.
The Lord make His face shine on you
and be gracious to you.
The Lord look upon you with favor
and give you peace.
People: Amen.

RECONCILIATION

SONG

> Leader: Simon Peter asked Jesus, "Lord, how often shall my brother sin against me and I forgive him? As many as seven times?"
>
> **People: Jesus said to him, "I do not say to you seven times, but seventy times seven."**

SCRIPTURE READING (Matthew 18:23-35)

MESSAGE

> Leader: Every time we try to deal with our sins by ignoring them or making excuses or running away, we end up worse than before.
>
> **People: But when we face our failures honestly and confess them to God, He will forgive (Psalm 32).**
> *(A time of silence for personal reflection and confession.)*
> **We confess that we have sinned against God our Creator and that we have sinned against the people around us by unkind words we have spoken and by unloving actions we have done.**
>
> Leader: Jesus came into the world and obeyed God's laws perfectly for you. He died on the cross for the guilt of your sins. Because of His great sacrifice, you are forgiven. And you are to forgive one another.

SONG "Lamb of God, You Take Away"

OFFERING

PRAYERS *(optional)*

LORD'S PRAYER

BENEDICTION

PRAYER

SONG

Leader: Grace to you and peace from God our Father and the Lord Jesus Christ.
People: Amen.

Leader: This is the day which the Lord has made;
People: let us rejoice and be glad in it.
Leader: From the rising of the sun to its setting
People: the name of the Lord is to be praised.
Leader: Have no anxiety about anything,
People: but in everything by prayer let your requests be made known to God.
Leader: They who wait for the Lord shall renew their strength;
People: they shall mount up with wings like eagles;
Leader: they shall run and not be weary;
People: they shall walk and not faint.

(Quiet for a time of reflection.)

SCRIPTURE READING

MESSAGE

PRAYERS

Leader: Almighty God, because You have committed Your people to the ministry of intercession, hear us as we pray for one another.
People: Fill our hearts with peace and love.
Leader: We pray for the world: Lord of all, we pray for Your whole creation. Enable us to bring an end to violence and injustice, to feed and clothe people and to be faithful caretakers of the earth, so that all may enjoy the good world which You have made. In Your mercy,
People: hear us, good Lord.
Leader: We pray for the Church: Heavenly Father, be with Your Church, give all ministers of the Word Your grace and truth that Your people might grow in faith, and that Christ may be honored by all. In Your mercy,
People: hear us, good Lord.
Leader: We pray for those who are ill, especially . . . : Source of all healing, we ask You to strengthen the tired, to ease the pain of those who

suffer, and to let those who are dying know that You hold them in Your loving arms. In Your mercy,

People: hear us, good Lord.

Leader: We pray for family and friends: O God our Father, bless those we love, and help us to love all people so that, as You love us, we may grow in love for each other. In Your mercy,

People: hear us, good Lord.

(*Other petitions may be added.*)

Leader: Almighty God, You have given us the grace to make our prayers known to You and have promised always to listen. Fulfill our requests as may be best and grant us knowledge of Your truth in this world and in the life to come. Through Jesus Christ, Your Son, our Lord.

People: Amen.

Leader: Lord, remember us in Your kingdom and teach us to pray:

People: Our Father, who art in heaven . . . .

BLESSING

Leader: The peace of God, which passes all understanding, keep your hearts and minds in the knowledge and love of God, and of His Son Jesus Christ, our Lord; and the blessing of God Almighty, the Father, the ✛ Son, and the Holy Spirit, be among you and remain with you always.

People: Amen.

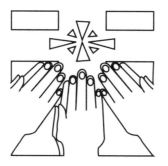

CREEDS AND PRAYERS

The Apostles' Creed

I believe in God, the Father Almighty,
    maker of heaven and earth.
And in Jesus Christ, His only Son, our Lord,
    who was conceived by the Holy Spirit,
    born of the Virgin Mary,
    suffered under Pontius Pilate,
    was crucified, died and was buried.
    He descended into hell.
    The third day He rose again from the dead.
    He ascended into heaven
        and sits at the right hand of God
        the Father Almighty.
From thence He will come to judge the living and the dead.

I believe in the Holy Spirit,
    the holy Christian Church,
    the communion of saints,
    the forgiveness of sins,
    the resurrection of the body,
    and the life everlasting. Amen.

Lord's Prayer

Our Father, who art in heaven,
    hallowed be Thy name,
    Thy kingdom come,
    Thy will be done
        on earth as it is in heaven.
Give us this day our daily bread;
and forgive us our trespasses
    as we forgive those
        who trespass against us;
and lead us not into temptation,
    but deliver us from evil.
For Thine is the kingdom
    and the power and the glory
    forever and ever. Amen.

OR

Our Father in heaven,
    hallowed be Your name,
    Your kingdom come,
    Your will be done
        on earth as in heaven.
Give us today our daily bread.
Forgive us our sins
    as we forgive those
        who sin against us.
Lead us not into temptation,
    but deliver us from evil.
For the kingdom, the power,
    and the glory are Yours
    now and forever. Amen.

Luther's Morning Prayer

I thank You, my heavenly Father, through Jesus Christ, Your dear Son, that You have kept me this night from all harm and danger; and I pray that You would keep me this day also from sin and every evil, that all my doings and life may please You. For into Your hands I commend myself, my body and soul, and all things. Let Your holy angel be with me, that the evil foe may have no power over me. Amen.

Luther's Evening Prayer

I thank You, my heavenly Father, through Jesus Christ, Your dear Son, that You have graciously kept me this day; and I pray that You would forgive me all my sins where I have done wrong, and graciously keep me this night. For into Your hands I commend myself, my body and soul, and all things. Let Your holy angel be with me, that the evil foe may have no power over me. Amen.

Advent

Dear heavenly Father, by the sending of Your Son, Jesus, You kept Your promise to a people long ago. We too thank You that Jesus became like us to save us from our sins, from death, and from the power of the devil. Make us able to live each day waiting for Jesus to come again and to take us to Himself in heaven. Hear us for our Savior's sake. Amen.

Christmas

Dear Father in heaven, thank You for the Gift of Christmas—Jesus, Your Son! With the shepherds we too bring our gifts——our love, our hearts, hands, and voices, our faith, and our lives to honor Him. Help us to share Your love all year long. Amen.

Epiphany

Praise and honor to You, heavenly Father, for offering the promises of Your love to all people in the world.

Praise and honor to You, dear Jesus, for being the Light of the whole world.

Praise and honor to You, Holy Spirit, for blessing the work of pastors, teachers, and missionaries and for bringing people everywhere into the Christian family.

Make us glad for the oneness we share with others in You. Enable us to shine like stars, pointing others to You. Amen.

Lent

Dear heavenly Father, through Baptism You have made us Your own children. During this Lenten time, cleanse our hearts that we might be truly sorry for our sinful nature. Send Your Spirit to us that we may learn of Your intent for our lives. Make us more generous in our showing of Your love to others. For the sake of our dear Savior we ask these things. Amen.

Holy Week

Almighty and eternal God, it was Your will that Your Son should suffer and die on the cross for us. May we always be thankful for Jesus' great work of love. Give us strength to follow His example of humility. Finally, in our own last hour, give to us everlasting life with You at Your heavenly throne. In Jesus' name we pray. Amen.

Easter

Lord Jesus, You have conquered sin and death and given to us eternal life. Fill our days with the wonderful joy of Your resurrection! Stay with us and with Your whole Church. May Your Word always be our strength and blessing. Amen.

Pentecost

Dear Jesus, before You ascended into heaven, You promised to send the Holy Spirit to be with Your people on earth. We are thankful for the gift of faith worked in us by Your Spirit and the gifts of joy, love, and peace. May the Holy Spirit strengthen, unite, and enlarge Your Church with all needful gifts that Your holy name be proclaimed to all nations on the earth. Trusting in Your mercy, we pray. Amen.

Evangelism/Mission

Dear Jesus, we remember Your command to make all people Your disciples. Enable us to spread Your Word throughout our neighborhood and beyond. Bless the missionaries and their families all around the world. Take care of them. Give them joy in their work. Be with all who share Your love. Amen.

Church

Heavenly Father, in Your Church You have given to us a great big family! Be with all pastors, teachers, and all others who labor in Your name. May Your light be on us as we listen to Your Word. Hear the prayers we offer and send Your Holy Spirit to guide us. May we always show love for one another in the name of Your Son, Jesus. Amen.

Home/Family

Dear Lord, we give You thanks for the gift of our family. Give us Your kind of love for one another. Help us to be forgiving, kind, and true. Especially we ask that You would keep us close to You. Give us joy in the reading of Your Word and in our times of praising You together. Protect us in times of danger, and keep our trust always in You. Come, Lord Jesus, be our Guest! Amen.

Nation

Lord of all nations, we thank You for our country. Bless the people of our land with those things they need for daily living. Give guidance to our leaders that Your will be done. Protect us at all times and give to us peace. In Jesus' name. Amen.

For the Sick

Lord Jesus, our Creator and Keeper, we remember _____ who is sick (hurt). Be with those who tend to him (her). Strengthen his (her) family and friends in this time. Remind them of Your great love and care for us. If it be Your will, restore to them sound health of body, soul, and mind. Hear our prayer for Your name's sake. Amen.

Word

Dear heavenly Father, You have given us a great gift in Your Holy Word. Make us attentive as we listen to it and study it. Make clear for us Your will for our lives. Hear us for Jesus' sake. Amen.

The Good Shepherd

Lord Jesus, You are the Good Shepherd. We know Your voice. You have laid down Your life for us. Attend to us in the green pastures of Your love that we may grow in knowledge, faith, and holiness. Protect us. When we stray, use Your Holy Spirit to bring us back into the fold. Keep us faithful and let us live with You forever in heaven. Amen.

Boldness in Witness

Dear Lord, You are our Savior and King. You always forgive us when we do wrong or fail to do what is right. Keep us humble, trusting in Your grace and mercy. But make us bold too; bold to live for You by serving others, bold to speak Your Word, bold to be known as Christians wherever we go. Teach us those truths You want us to know. We pray in Jesus' name. Amen.

Litany 1

Leader: Dear Lord, You have invited us to pray about everything. We believe Your promise to hear the prayers we offer in Jesus' name. We pray, Lord, that You would give us mercy and forgive our sins by which we have offended You:

People: Lord, hear our prayer.

Leader: Bring an end to quarreling and fighting among us and among the peoples of the earth. Give us grace to live together in peace:

People: Lord, hear our prayer.

Leader: Help us work and play in such a way that all our activities may bring honor to Your name.

People: Lord, hear our prayer.

Leader: Watch over the sick, the troubled, the lonely people of the world, and let them experience the strength and joy Your Spirit gives.

People: Lord, hear our prayer.

Leader: Give peace to our nation; protect us from war and violence, and give us hope in times of disaster:

People: Lord, hear our prayer.

Leader: Bless our church and school, our pastor and teachers, and all others who serve in this place:

People: Lord, hear our prayer.

Leader: Guard our homes and families with Your love, and make us loving and considerate of one another:

People: Lord, hear our prayer.

Leader: All these blessings we are bold to ask because You have given us the greatest blessing of all——Yourself. We would give You our selves. We love because You first loved us.

People: Amen.

Litany 2

Leader: In the name of our God——Father, Son, and Holy Spirit. Amen. For making the world and all that is in it good:

People: Thank You, God.

Leader: For making us and giving us wonderful bodies and minds:

People: Thank You, God.

Leader: For wanting us to be happy and to enjoy the world You made:

People: Thank You, God.

Leader: For the homes we have and the people who love and care for us:

People: Thank You, God.

Leader: For food to eat and people who prepare it:

People: Thank You, God.

Leader: For friends with whom we work and play:

People: Thank You, God.

Leader: For leading us to know You are our Friend and Savior:

People: Thank You, God.

Leader: For Baptism and for the gift of the Holy Spirit:

People: Thank You, God.

Leader: For everything:

People: Thank You, God. Amen.

DR. MARTIN LUTHER'S SMALL CATECHISM

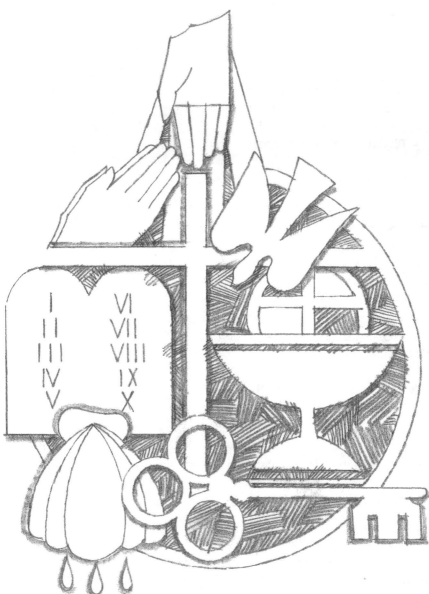

The Ten Commandments

The First Commandment

You shall have no other gods.

What does this mean? We should fear, love, and trust in God above all things.

The Second Commandment

You shall not misuse the name of the Lord your God.

What does this mean? We should fear and love God so that we do not curse, swear, use satanic arts, lie, or deceive by His name, but call upon it in every trouble, pray, praise, and give thanks.

The Third Commandment

Remember the Sabbath day by keeping it holy.

What does this mean? We should fear and love God so that we do not despise preaching and His Word, but hold it sacred and gladly hear and learn it.

The Fourth Commandment

Honor your father and your mother.

What does this mean? We should fear and love God so that we do not despise or anger our parents and other authorities, but honor them, serve and obey them, love and cherish them.

The Fifth Commandment

You shall not murder.

What does this mean? We should fear and love God so that we do not hurt or harm our neighbor in his body, but help and support him in every physical need.

The Sixth Commandment

You shall not commit adultery.

What does this mean? We should fear and love God so that we lead a sexually pure and decent life in what we say and do, and husband and wife love and honor each other.

The Seventh Commandment

You shall not steal.

What does this mean? We should fear and love God so that we do not take our neighbor's money or possessions, or get them in any dishonest way, but help him to improve and protect his possessions and income.

The Eighth Commandment

You shall not give false testimony against your neighbor.

What does this mean? We should fear and love God so that we do not tell lies about our neighbor, betray him, slander him, or hurt his reputation, but defend him, speak well of him, and explain everything in the kindest way.

The Ninth Commandment

You shall not covet your neighbor's house.

What does this mean? We should fear and love God so that we do not scheme to get our neighbor's inheritance or house, or get it in a way which only appears right, but help and be of service to him in keeping it.

The Tenth Commandment

You shall not covet your neighbor's wife, or his manservant or maidservant, his ox or donkey, or anything that belongs to your neighbor.

What does this mean? We should fear and love God so that we do not entice or force away our neighbor's wife, workers, or animals, or turn them against him, but urge them to stay and do their duty.

[Text of the commandments is from Exodus 20:3a, 7a, 8, 12–17.]

The Close of the Commandments

What does God say about all these commandments?

He says:"I, the Lord your God, am a jealous God, punishing the children for the sin of the fathers to the third and fourth generation of those who hate Me, but showing love to a thousand generations of those who love Me and keep my commandments." *[Exodus 20:5–6]*

What does this mean? God threatens to punish all who break these commandments. Therefore, we should fear His wrath and not do anything against them. But He promises grace and every blessing to all who keep these commandments. Therefore, we should also love and trust in Him and gladly do what He commands.

The Creed

The First Article

Creation

I believe in God, the Father Almighty, Maker of heaven and earth.

What does this mean? I believe that God has made me and all creatures; that He has given me my body and soul, eyes, ears, and all my members, my reason and all my senses, and still takes care of them.

He also gives me clothing and shoes, food and drink, house and home, wife and children, land, animals, and all I have. He richly and daily provides me with all that I need to support this body and life.

He defends me against all danger and guards and protects me from all evil.

All this He does only out of fatherly, divine goodness and mercy, without any merit or worthiness in me. For all this it is my duty to thank and praise, serve and obey Him.

This is most certainly true.

The Second Article

Redemption

And in Jesus Christ, His only Son, our Lord, who was conceived by the Holy Spirit, born of the Virgin Mary, suffered under Pontius Pilate, was crucified, died and was buried. He descended into hell. The third day He rose again from the dead. He ascended into heaven and sits at the right hand of God the Father Almighty. From thence He will come to judge the living and the dead.

What does this mean? I believe that Jesus Christ, true God, begotten of the Father from eternity, and also true man, born of the Virgin Mary, is my Lord,

who has redeemed me, a lost and condemned person, purchased and won me from all sins, from death, and from the power of the devil; not with gold or silver, but with His holy, precious blood and with His innocent suffering and death,

that I may be His own, and live under Him in His kingdom and serve Him in everlasting righteousness, innocence, and blessedness,

just as He is risen from the dead, lives and reigns to all eternity.

This is most certainly true.

The Third Article

Sanctification

I believe in the Holy Spirit, the holy Christian Church, the communion of saints, the forgiveness of sins, the resurrection of the body, and the life everlasting. Amen.

What does this mean? I believe that I cannot by my own reason or strength believe in Jesus Christ, my Lord, or come to Him; but the Holy Spirit has called me by the Gospel, enlightened me with His gifts, sanctified and kept me in the true faith.

In the same way He calls, gathers, enlightens, and sanctifies the whole Christian Church on earth, and keeps it with Jesus Christ in the one true faith.

In this Christian Church He daily and richly forgives all my sins and the sins of all believers.

On the Last Day He will raise me and all the dead, and give eternal life to me and all believers in Christ.

This is most certainly true.

The Lord's Prayer

Our Father who art in heaven,
   hallowed be Thy name,
   Thy kingdom come,
   Thy will be done
      on earth as it is in heaven.
Give us this day our daily bread;
and forgive us our trespasses
   as we forgive those
      who trespass against us;
and lead us not into temptation,
   but deliver us from evil.
For Thine is the kingdom
   and the power and the glory
   forever and ever. Amen.

Our Father in heaven,
   hallowed be Your name,
   Your kingdom come,
   Your will be done
      on earth as in heaven.
Give us today our daily bread.
Forgive us our sins
   as we forgive those
      who sin against us.
Lead us not into temptation,
   but deliver us from evil.
For the kingdom, the power,
   and the glory are Yours
   now and forever. Amen.

The Introduction

Our Father who art in heaven.

Our Father in heaven.

What does this mean? With these words God tenderly invites us to believe that He is our true Father and that we are His true children, so that with all boldness and confidence we may ask Him as dear children ask their dear father.

The First Petition

Hallowed be Thy name.

Hallowed be Your name.

What does this mean? God's name is certainly holy in itself, but we pray in this petition that it may be kept holy among us also.

How is God's name kept holy? God's name is kept holy when the Word of God is taught in its truth and purity, and we, as the children of God, also lead holy lives according to it. Help us to do this, dear Father in heaven! But anyone who teaches or lives contrary to God's Word profanes the name of God among us. Protect us from this, heavenly Father!

The Second Petition

Thy kingdom come.

Your kingdom come.

What does this mean? The kingdom of God certainly comes by itself without our prayer, but we pray in this petition that it may come to us also.

How does God's kingdom come? God's kingdom comes when our heavenly Father gives us His Holy Spirit, so that by His grace we believe His holy Word and lead godly lives here in time and there in eternity.

The Third Petition

Thy will be done on earth as it is in heaven.

Your will be done on earth as in heaven.

What does this mean? The good and gracious will of God is done even without our prayer, but we pray in this petition that it may be done among us also.

How is God's will done? God's will is done when He breaks and hinders every evil plan and purpose of the devil, the world, and our sinful nature, which do not want us to hallow God's name or let His kingdom come; and when He strengthens and keeps us firm in His Word and faith until we die. This is His good and gracious will.

The Fourth Petition

Give us this day our daily bread.

Give us today our daily bread.

What does this mean? God certainly gives daily bread to everyone without our prayers, even to all evil people, but we pray in this petition that God would lead us to realize this and to receive our daily bread with thanksgiving.

What is meant by daily bread? Daily bread includes everything that has to do with the support and needs of the body, such as food, drink, clothing, shoes, house, home, land, animals, money, goods, a devout husband or wife, devout children, devout workers, devout and faithful rulers, good government, good weather, peace, health, self–control, good reputation, good friends, faithful neighbors, and the like.

The Fifth Petition

And forgive us our trespasses, as we forgive those who trespass against us.

Forgive us our sins as we forgive those who sin against us.

What does this mean? We pray in this petition that our Father in heaven would not look at our sins, or deny our prayer because of them. We are neither worthy of the things for which we pray, nor have we deserved them, but we ask that He would give them all to us by grace, for we daily sin much and surely deserve nothing but punishment. So we too will sincerely forgive and gladly do good to those who sin against us.

The Sixth Petition

And lead us not into temptation.

Lead us not into temptation.

What does this mean? God tempts no one. We pray in this petition that God would guard and keep us so that the devil, the world, and our sinful nature may not deceive us or mislead us into false belief, despair, and other great shame and vice. Although we are attacked by these things, we pray that we may finally overcome them and win the victory.

The Seventh Petition

But deliver us from evil.

But deliver us from evil.

What does this mean? We pray in this petition, in summary, that our Father in heaven would rescue us from every evil of body and soul, possessions and reputation, and finally, when our last hour comes, give us a blessed end, and graciously take us from this valley of sorrow to Himself in heaven.

The Conclusion

For Thine is the kingdom and the power and the glory forever and ever.* Amen.

For the kingdom, the power, and the glory are Yours now and forever. * Amen.

What does this mean? This means that I should be certain that these petitions are pleasing to our Father in heaven, and are heard by Him; for He Himself has commanded us to pray in this way and has promised to hear us. Amen, amen, means "yes, yes, it shall be so."

* These words were not in Luther's Small Catechism.

The Sacrament of Holy Baptism

First

What is Baptism?

Baptism is not just plain water, but it is the water included in God's command and combined with God's word.

Which is that word of God?

Christ our Lord says in the last chapter of Matthew: "Therefore go and make disciples of all nations, baptizing them in the name of the Father and of the Son and of the Holy Spirit." [*Matthew 28:19*]

Second

What benefits does Baptism give?

It works forgiveness of sins, rescues from death and the devil, and gives eternal salvation to all who believe this, as the words and promises of God declare.

Which are these words and promises of God?

Christ our Lord says in the last chapter of Mark: "Whoever believes and is baptized will be saved, but whoever does not believe will be condemned." [*Mark 16:16*]

Third

How can water do such great things?

Certainly not just water, but the word of God in and with the water does these things, along with the faith which trusts this word of God in the water. For without God's word the water is plain water and no Baptism. But with the word of God it is a Baptism, that is, a life–giving water, rich in grace, and a washing of the new birth in the Holy Spirit, as St. Paul says in Titus, chapter three: "He saved us through the washing of rebirth and renewal by the Holy Spirit, whom He poured out on us generously through Jesus Christ our Savior, so that, having been justified by His grace, we might become heirs having the hope of eternal life. This is a trustworthy saying." [*Titus 3:5b–8a*]

Fourth

What does such baptizing with water indicate?

It indicates that the Old Adam in us should by daily contrition and repentance be drowned and die with all sins and evil desires, and that a new man should daily emerge and arise to live before God in righteousness and purity forever.

Where is this written?

St. Paul writes in Romans chapter six: "We were therefore buried with Him through baptism into death in order that, just as Christ was raised from the dead through the glory of the Father, we too may live a new life." [*Romans 6:4*]

Confession

What is Confession?

Confession has two parts.

First, that we confess our sins, and

second, that we receive absolution, that is, forgiveness, from the pastor as from God Himself, not doubting, but firmly believing that by it our sins are forgiven before God in heaven.

What sins should we confess?

Before God we should plead guilty of all sins, even those we are not aware of, as we do in the Lord's Prayer; but before the pastor we should confess only those sins which we know and feel in our hearts.

Which are these?

Consider your place in life according to the Ten Commandments: Are you a father, mother, son, daughter, husband, wife, or worker? Have you been disobedient, unfaithful, or lazy? Have you been hot–tempered, rude, or quarrelsome? Have you hurt someone by your words or deeds? Have you stolen, been negligent, wasted anything, or done any harm?

What is the Office of the Keys?

The Office of the Keys is that special authority which Christ has given to His Church on earth to forgive the sins of repentant sinners, but to withhold forgiveness from the unrepentant as long as they do not repent.

Where is this written?

This is what St. John the Evangelist writes in chapter twenty: "The Lord Jesus breathed on His disciples and said, 'Receive the Holy Spirit. If you forgive anyone his sins, they are forgiven; if you do not forgive them, they are not forgiven.'" [*John 20:22–23*]

What do you believe according to these words?

I believe that when the called ministers of Christ deal with us by His divine command, in particular when they exclude openly unrepentant sinners from the Christian congregation and absolve those who repent of their sins and want to do better, this is just as valid and certain, even in heaven, as if Christ our dear Lord dealt with us Himself.

The Sacrament of the Altar

What is the Sacrament of the Altar?

It is the true body and blood of our Lord Jesus Christ under the bread and wine, instituted by Christ Himself for us Christians to eat and to drink.

Where is this written?

The holy Evangelists Matthew, Mark, Luke, and St. Paul write:
Our Lord Jesus Christ, on the night when He was betrayed, took bread, and when He had given thanks, He broke it and gave it to the disciples and said: "Take, eat; this is My body, which is given for you. This do in remembrance of Me."
In the same way also He took the cup after supper, and when He had given thanks, He gave it to them, saying, "Drink of it, all of you; this cup is the new testament in My blood, which is shed for you for the forgiveness of sins. This do, as often as you drink it, in remembrance of Me."

What is the benefit of this eating and drinking?

These words, "Given and shed for you for the forgiveness of sins," show us that in the Sacrament forgiveness of sins, life, and salvation are given us through these words. For where there is forgiveness of sins, there is also life and salvation.

How can bodily eating and drinking do such great things?

Certainly not just eating and drinking does these things, but the words written here: "Given and shed for you for the forgiveness of sins." These words, along with the bodily eating and drinking, are the main thing in the Sacrament. Whoever believes these words has exactly what they say: "forgiveness of sins."

Who receives this Sacrament worthily?

Fasting and bodily preparation are certainly fine outward training. But that person is truly worthy and well–prepared who has faith in these words: "Given and shed for you for the forgiveness of sins."
But anyone who does not believe these words or doubts them is unworthy and unprepared, for the words "for you" require all hearts to believe.

HYMNS AND SONGS

50 A Mighty Fortress Is Our God

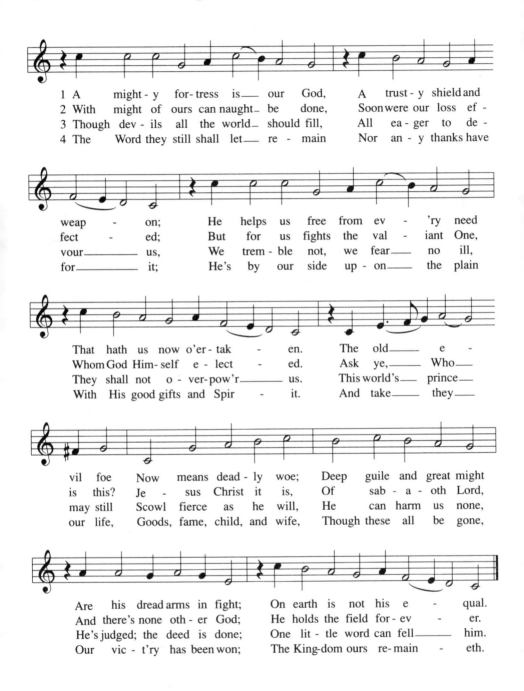

1 A might-y for-tress is— our God, A trust-y shield and
2 With might of ours can naught— be done, Soon were our loss ef -
3 Though dev - ils all the world— should fill, All ea - ger to de -
4 The Word they still shall let— re - main Nor an - y thanks have

weap - on; He helps us free from ev - 'ry need
fect - ed; But for us fights the val - iant One,
vour— us, We trem - ble not, we fear— no ill,
for— it; He's by our side up - on— the plain

That hath us now o'er - tak - en. The old— e -
Whom God Him- self e - lect - ed. Ask ye,— Who—
They shall not o - ver-pow'r— us. This world's— prince—
With His good gifts and Spir - it. And take— they—

vil foe Now means dead - ly woe; Deep guile and great might
is this? Je - sus Christ it is, Of sab - a - oth Lord,
may still Scowl fierce as he will, He can harm us none,
our life, Goods, fame, child, and wife, Though these all be gone,

Are his dread arms in fight; On earth is not his e - qual.
And there's none oth - er God; He holds the field for - ev - er.
He's judged; the deed is done; One lit - tle word can fell— him.
Our vic - t'ry has been won; The King-dom ours re - main - eth.

Text: Martin Luther, 1483-1546; tr. composite
Tune: **Ein feste Burg** *(rhythmic), Martin Luther, 1483-1546*

A Mighty Fortress Is Our God

1 A might-y for-tress is our God, A sword and shield vic-to-rious; He breaks the cruel op-pres-sor's rod And wins sal-va-tion glo-rious. The old sa-tan-ic foe Has sworn to work us woe. With craft and dread-ful might He arms him-self to fight. On earth he has no e-qual.

2 No strength of ours can match His might. We would be lost, re-ject-ed. But now a cham-pion comes to fight, Whom God Him-self e-lect-ed. You ask who this may be? The Lord of hosts is He, Christ Je-sus, might-y Lord, God's on-ly Son, a-dored. He holds the field vic-to-rious.

3 Though hordes of dev-ils fill the land All threat-'ning to de-vour us, We trem-ble not, un-moved we stand; They can-not o-ver-pow'r us. Let this world's ty-rant rage; In bat-tle we'll en-gage. His might is doomed to fail; God's judg-ment must pre-vail! One lit-tle word sub-dues him.

4 God's Word for-ev-er shall a-bide, No thanks to foes, who fear it; For God Him-self fights by our side With weap-ons of the Spir-it. Were they to take our house, Goods, hon-or, child, or spouse, Though life be wrenched a-way, They can-not win the day. The King-dom's ours for-ev-er!

Text: Martin Luther, 1483-1546; tr. Lutheran Book of Worship, *1978*
Tune: **Ein feste Burg** *(isorhythmic), Martin Luther, 1483-1546.*

52 A Stable Lamp Is Lighted

1 A sta - ble lamp is light - ed Whose
2 child through Da - vid's cit - y Shall
3 He shall be for - sak - en, And
4 now, as at the end - ing, The

glow shall wake the sky; The stars shall blend their
ride in tri - umph by; The palm shall strew its
yield - ed up to die; The sky shall groan and
low is lift - ed high; The stars shall blend their

voic - es, And ev - 'ry stone shall cry. And ev - 'ry stone shall
branch-es, And ev - 'ry stone shall cry. And ev - 'ry stone shall
dark - en, And ev - 'ry stone shall cry. And ev - 'ry stone shall
voic - es, And ev - 'ry stone shall cry. And ev - 'ry stone shall

cry, And straw like gold shall shine; A
cry, Though heav - y, dull, and dumb, And
cry, For hearts made hard by sin: God's
cry, In prais - es of the child By

barn shall har - bor heav - en, A stall be - come a
lie with - in the road - way To pave the king - dom
blood up - on the spear - head, God's love re - fused a -
whose de - scent a - mong us The worlds are rec - on -

shrine.   This
come.   Yet
gain.   But
ciled.

53

A Time to Serve

1 Je - sus hears His chil - dren cry - ing, Sees them
2 Je - sus pleads with us to reach them With our
3 Young and old a - like He's call - ing, Hu - man
4 When we join our Sav - ior's serv - ice, He will

hun - gry, lost, and dy - ing; Who will com - fort all their
gifts of love, and teach them That the kind - ness we are
grief is so ap - pall - ing; Since He gave His life to
strength - en and pre - serve us; He will guide our dai - ly

sor - rows? Who will bright - en their to - mor - rows?
giv - ing Is the Chris - tian's way of liv - ing.
save us, Let us share the lives He gave us.
liv - ing, And He'll bless the love we're giv - ing.

5 When we aid the poor and lonely,
We're not caring for them only;
When our love some suff'ring eases,
We have done the same for Jesus.

6 Rise and follow! He will lead us;
Heed the cries of those who need us!
And when life has ended for us,
Heaven's glories lie before us.

©Text: Robert Baden
Tune: **Tryggare kan ingen vara**, Swedish folk tune

Abide with Me

54

1 A - bide with me, fast falls the e - ven - tide.
2 I need Thy pres - ence ev - 'ry pass - ing hour;
3 I fear no foe with Thee at hand to bless;
4 Hold Thou Thy cross be - fore my clos - ing eyes,

The dark - ness deep - ens; Lord, with me a - bide.
What but Thy grace can foil the tempt - er's pow'r?
Ills have no weight, and tears no bit - ter - ness.
Shine through the gloom, and point me to the skies;

When oth - er help - ers fail and com - forts flee,
Who like Thy - self my guide and stay can be?
Where is death's sting? Where, grave, thy vic - to - ry?
Heav'n's morn - ing breaks, and earth's vain shad - ows flee;

Help of the help - less, oh, a - bide with me.
Through cloud and sun - shine, oh, a - bide with me.
I tri - umph still if Thou a - bide with me!
In life, in death, O Lord, a - bide with me.

Text: Henry F. Lyte, 1793-1847
*Tune: **Eventide**, William H. Monk, 1823-89*

55   Abide with Us, Our Savior

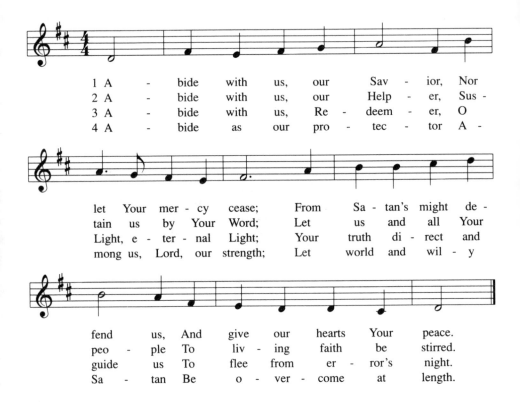

1 A - bide with us, our Sav - ior, Nor
2 A - bide with us, our Help - er, Sus -
3 A - bide with us, Re - deem - er, O
4 A - bide as our pro - tec - tor A -

let Your mer - cy cease; From Sa - tan's might de -
tain us by Your Word; Let us and all Your
Light, e - ter - nal Light; Your truth di - rect and
mong us, Lord, our strength; Let world and wil - y

fend us, And give our hearts Your peace.
peo - ple To liv - ing faith be stirred.
guide us To flee from er - ror's night.
Sa - tan Be o - ver - come at length.

5 Abide among us always,
  O Lord, our faithful Friend,
  And take us to Your mansions
  When time and world shall end.

Text: *Josua Stegmann, 1558-1632; tr. composite, alt.*
Tune: **Christus, der ist mein Leben**, *Melchior Vulpius, c. 1560-1615*

All Hail the Power of Jesus' Name 56

1 All hail the pow'r of Je-sus' name! Let an-gels pros-trate
2 O seed of Is-rael's cho-sen race, Now ran-somed from the
3 Let ev-'ry kin-dred, ev-'ry tribe On this ter-res-tr'al
4 Oh, that with yon-der sa-cred throng We at His feet may

fall; Bring forth the roy-al di - a - dem And
fall, Hail Him who saves you by His grace And
ball To Him all maj - es - ty as - cribe And
fall! We'll join the ev - er - last - ing song And

crown Him Lord of___ all. Bring forth the roy - al
crown Him Lord of___ all. Hail Him who saves you
crown Him Lord of___ all. To Him all maj - es -
crown Him Lord of___ all. We'll join the ev - er -

di - a - dem And crown Him Lord____ of all.
by His grace And crown Him Lord____ of all.
ty as - cribe And crown Him Lord____ of all.
last - ing song And crown Him Lord____ of all.

Text: Edward Perronet, 1716-92, sts. 1-2, alt.; John Rippon, A Selection of Hymns, *1787, sts. 3-4, alt.*
Tune: **Coronation,** *Oliver Holden, 1765-1844*

57 All Praise to Thee, My God, This Night

1 All praise to Thee, my God, this night For all the bless-ings of the light. Keep me, oh, keep me, King of kings, Be-neath Thine own al-might-y wings.

2 For-give me, Lord, for Thy dear Son, The ill that I this day have done; That with the world, my-self, and Thee, I, ere I sleep, at peace may be.

3 Teach me to live that I may dread The grave as lit-tle as my bed. Teach me to die that so I may Rise glo-rious at the awe-some day.

4 Praise God, from whom all bless-ings flow; Praise Him, all crea-tures here be-low; Praise Him a-bove, ye heav'n-ly host; Praise Fa-ther, Son, and Ho-ly Ghost.

Text: Thomas Ken, 1637-1711
Tune: **Tallis' Canon,** *Thomas Tallis, c. 1505-85*

All Things Work Out for Good

58

1 All things work out for good, we know—Such
2 This is the faith that keeps me still, No
3 So now the fu - ture holds no fear, God
4 Some day the path He chose for me Will

is God's great de - sign; He or - ders all our
mat - ter what the test, And lets me glo - ry
guards the work be - gun; And mor - tals are im -
all be un - der - stood; In heav - en's clear - er

steps be - low For pur - pos - es di - vine.
in His will— For well I know 'tis best.
mor - tal here Un - til their work is done.
light I'll see All things worked out for good.

Text: John W. Peterson
Tune: **St. Peter**, *Alexander R. Reinagle, 1799-1877*

59

Alleluia

1 Al - le - lu - ia, al - le - lu - ia,
2 How I love Him, how I love Him,
3 Bless-ed Je - sus, bless-ed Je - sus,
4 My re - deem - er, my re - deem - er,
5 Je - sus is Lord, Je - sus is Lord,
6 Al - le - lu - ia, al - le - lu - ia,

al - le - lu - ia, al - le - lu - ia,
how I love Him, how I love Him.
bless-ed Je - sus, bless-ed Je - sus,
my re - deem - er, my re - deem - er,
Je - sus is Lord, Je - sus is Lord,
al - le - lu - ia, al - le - lu - ia,

al - le - lu - ia.
how I love Him.
bless - ed Je - sus.
my re - deem - er.
Je - sus is Lord.
al - le - lu - ia.

Text: Jerry Sinclair
Tune: Jerry Sinclair

60

Alleluia! Sing to Jesus

1 Al - le - lu - ia! Sing to Je - sus;
2 Al - le - lu - ia! Not as or - phans
3 Al - le - lu - ia! Bread of heav - en,
4 Al - le - lu - ia! Sing to Je - sus;

His the scep - ter, His the throne;
Are we left in sor - row now;
Here on earth our food, our stay;
His the scep - ter, His the throne;

Al - le - lu - ia! His the tri - umph,
Al - le - lu - ia! He is near us;
Al - le - lu - ia! Here the sin - ful
Al - le - lu - ia! His the tri - umph,

His the vic - to - ry a - lone.
Faith be - lieves, nor ques - tions how.
Flee to You from day to day.
His the vic - to - ry a - lone.

Hark! The songs of peace - ful Zi - on
Though the cloud from sight re - ceived Him
In - ter - ces - sor, friend of sin - ners,
Hark! The songs of peace - ful Zi - on

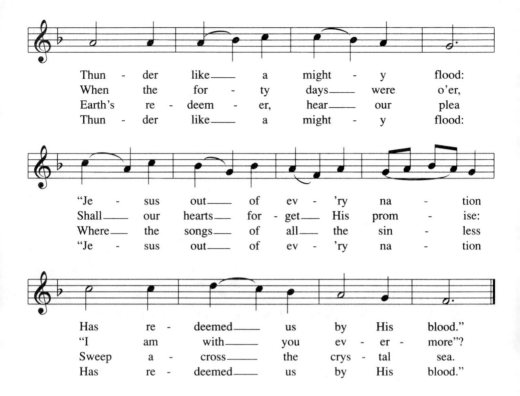

Thun - der like____ a might - y flood:
When the for - ty days____ were o'er,
Earth's re - deem - er, hear____ our plea
Thun - der like____ a might - y flood:

"Je - sus out____ of ev - 'ry na - tion
Shall____ our hearts____ for - get____ His prom - ise:
Where____ the songs____ of all____ the sin - less
"Je - sus out____ of ev - 'ry na - tion

Has re - deemed____ us by His blood."
"I am with____ you ev - er - more"?
Sweep a - cross____ the crys - tal sea.
Has re - deemed____ us by His blood."

Text: William C. Dix, 1837-1898; alt.
Tune: **Hyfrydol,** *Rowland H. Prichard, 1811-87*

61

Alleluia to Jesus

1 As Ja - cob with trav - el was wea - ry one day, At____
2 This lad - der is long, it is strong and well made, Has stood
3 Come let us as - cend! all may climb it who will; For the
4 And when we ar - rive at the ha - ven of rest, We shall

night on a stone for a pil - low he lay; He____
hun - dreds of years and is not yet de - cayed; Man - y
an - gels of Ja - cob are guard - ing it still: And re -
hear the glad words, "Come up hith - er, ye blest, Here are

saw in a vi - sion a lad - der so high That its
mil - lions have climbed it and reached Si - on's hill, And____
mem - ber, each step that by faith we pass o'er, Some____
re - gions of light, here are man - sions of bliss." O,____

foot was on earth and its top in the sky:
thou - sands by faith are____ climb - ing it still:
proph - et or mar - tyr hath trod it be - fore:
who would not climb such a lad - der as this?

Al- le - lu - ia to Je - sus, who died on the tree, And hath

raised up a lad - der of mer - cy for me, And hath

raised up a lad - der of mer - cy for me.

Text: traditional
Tune: **Jacob's Ladder,** *traditional*

62 Almighty God, Your Word Is Cast

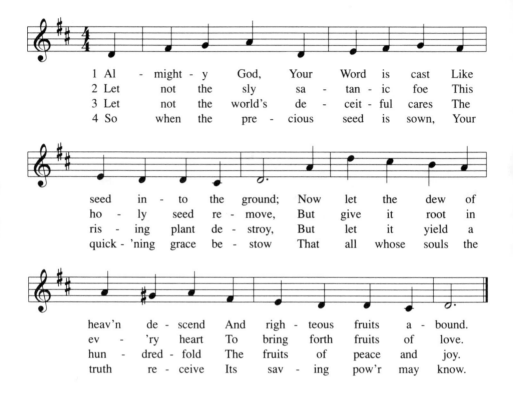

1 Al - might - y God, Your Word is cast Like
2 Let not the sly sa - tan - ic foe This
3 Let not the world's de - ceit - ful cares The
4 So when the pre - cious seed is sown, Your

seed in - to the ground; Now let the dew of
ho - ly seed re - move, But give it root in
ris - ing plant de - stroy, But let it yield a
quick - 'ning grace be - stow That all whose souls the

heav'n de - scend And righ - teous fruits a - bound.
ev - 'ry heart To bring forth fruits of love.
hun - dred - fold The fruits of peace and joy.
truth re - ceive Its sav - ing pow'r may know.

Text: John Cawood, 1775-1852; alt.
*Tune: **Dundee**, J. Day, Psalter, 1562*

Amazing Grace! How Sweet the Sound

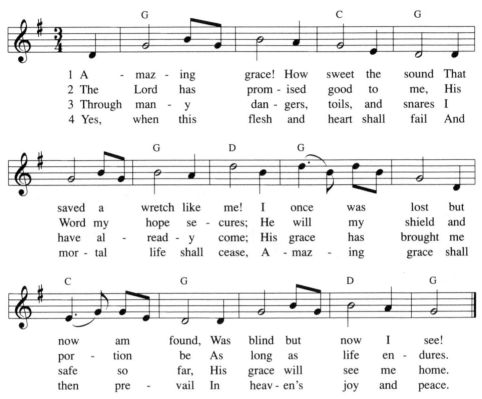

1 A - maz - ing grace! How sweet the sound That
2 The Lord has prom - ised good to me, His
3 Through man - y dan - gers, toils, and snares I
4 Yes, when this flesh and heart shall fail And

saved a wretch like me! I once was lost but
Word my hope se - cures; He will my shield and
have al - read - y come; His grace has brought me
mor - tal life shall cease, A - maz - ing grace shall

now am found, Was blind but now I see!
por - tion be As long as life en - dures.
safe so far, His grace will see me home.
then pre - vail In heav - en's joy and peace.

Text: John Newton, 1725-1807, alt.
*Tune: **New Britain**, J. Carrell and D. Clayton, Virginia Harmony, 1831*

64

Amigos de Cristo

Refrain

A - mi- gos de Cris-to; We're friends of the Lord, A -
A - mi- gos de Cris-to, de Cris - to, el Se - ñor, Por

mi- gos de Cris - to; We're friends of the Lord. For
él per - do - na - dos por su gran a - mor. A -

we've been for - giv - en And we've been re - stored! A -
mi - gos de Cris - to, de Cris - to el Se - ñor, Tam -

mi - gos de Cris - to; We're friends___ of the Lord!
bién res - tau - ra - dos por el Con - so - la - dor.

1 Friends of the cov - e - nant re - newed each morn,
2 Born of a fam - i - ly the young and old,

Bap - tized and lov - in' it, we've been re - born;
We'll be on hand to see new life un - fold;

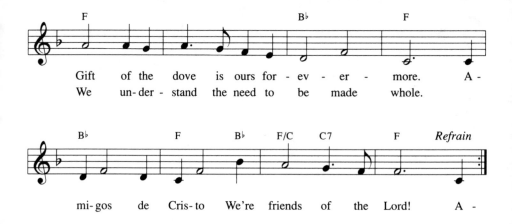

Gift of the dove is ours for - ev - er - more. A -
We un- der - stand the need to be made whole.

mi- gos de Cris- to We're friends of the Lord! A -

65 Angels We Have Heard on High

1 An - gels we have heard on high,
2 Shep - herds, why this ju - bi - lee?
3 Come to Beth - le - hem and see
4 Glo - ry to the Fa - ther be,

Sweet - ly sing - ing o'er the plains.
Why your joy - ous strains pro - long?
Him whose birth the an - gels sing:
Glo - ry, Vir - gin - born, to Thee,

And the moun - tains in re - ply
What the glad - some tid - ings be
Come, a - dore on bend - ed knee
Glo - ry to the Ho - ly Ghost,

Ech - o - ing their joy - ous strains:
Which in - spire your heav'n - ly song?
Christ the Lord, the new - born King.
Praised by men and heav'n - ly host:

Glo - - - ri - a in ex - cel - sis De - o! Glo - - - ri - a in ex - cel - sis De - o!

Text: French carol, tr. H. F. Hemy, *Crown of Jesus Part II, 1862,* alt.
Tune: **Gloria**, *traditional French carol*

66

At the Lamb's High Feast

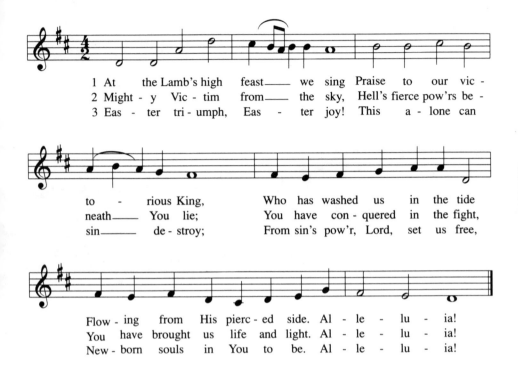

1 At the Lamb's high feast—— we sing Praise to our vic-
2 Might-y Vic-tim from—— the sky, Hell's fierce pow'rs be-
3 Eas-ter tri-umph, Eas-ter joy! This a-lone can

to-rious King, Who has washed us in the tide
neath—— You lie; You have con-quered in the fight,
sin—— de-stroy; From sin's pow'r, Lord, set us free,

Flow-ing from His pierc-ed side. Al-le-lu-ia!
You have brought us life and light. Al-le-lu-ia!
New-born souls in You to be. Al-le-lu-ia!

Text: office hymn, 17th cent.; tr. Robert Campbell, 1814-68, alt.
*Tune: **Sonne der Gerechitigkeit**, Bohemian Brethren, Kirchengeseng, 1566*

Away in a Manger

67

1 A - way in a man - ger, no crib for a
2 The cat - tle are low - ing, the ba - by a -
3 Be near me, Lord Je - sus; I ask Thee to

bed, The lit - tle Lord Je - sus laid down His sweet
wakes, But lit - tle Lord Je - sus, no cry - ing He
stay Close by me for - ev - er and love me, I

head. The stars in the bright sky looked down where He
makes. I love Thee, Lord Je - sus! Look down from the
pray. Bless all the dear chil - dren in Thy ten - der

lay, The lit - tle Lord Je - sus a - sleep on the hay.
sky, And stay by my side un - til morn - ing is nigh.
care, And take us to heav - en to live with Thee there.

Text: author unknown, c. 1883, sts. 1-2; John T. McFarland, 1851-1913, st. 3, alt.
Tune: American, 19th cent.

68

Away in a Manger

1 A - way in a man-ger, no crib for a
2 The cat - tle are low-ing, the ba - by a -
3 Be near me, Lord Je - sus; I ask Thee to

bed, The lit - tle Lord Je - sus laid down His sweet
wakes, But lit - tle Lord Je - sus, no cry - ing He
stay Close by me for - ev - er and love me, I

head. The stars in the bright sky looked down where He
makes. I love Thee, Lord Je - sus! Look down from the
pray. Bless all the dear chil - dren in Thy ten - der

lay, The lit - tle Lord Je - sus a - sleep on the hay.
sky, And stay by my side un - til morn - ing is nigh.
care, And take us to heav-en to live with Thee there.

Text: author unknown, c. 1883, sts. 1-2; John T. McFarland, 1851-1913, st. 3, alt.
*Tune: **Cradle Song**, William J. Kirkpatrick, 1838-1921*

Battle Hymn of the Republic

69

1 Mine_____ eyes have seen the glo - ry of the
2 He has sound - ed forth the trum - pet that shall
3 In the beau - ty of the lil - ies Christ was

com - ing of the Lord; He is tram-pling out the vin - tage where the
nev - er call re- treat; He is sift - ing out the hearts of men be -
born a- cross the sea, With a glo - ry in His bo - som that trans-

grapes of wrath are stored; He has loosed the fate - ful light-ning of His
fore His judg-ment seat. Oh, be swift, my soul, to an- swer Him; be
fig - ures you and me. As He died to make men ho - ly, let us

ter - ri - ble swift sword: His truth is march - ing on.
ju - bi - lant, my feet! Our God is march - ing on.
live to make men free, While God is march - ing on.

Glo - ry, glo-ry! Hal- le - lu - jah! Glo - ry, glo-ry! Hal- le - lu - jah!

Glo - ry, glo-ry! Hal- le - lu - jah! His truth is march- ing on.

Text: Julia Ward Howe, 1819-1910
*Tune: **Battle Hymn**, American, 19th cent.*

70

Beautiful Savior

1 Beau - ti - ful Sav - ior, King of cre - a - tion,
2 Fair are the mead - ows, Fair are the wood - lands,
3 Fair is the sun - shine, Fair is the moon - light,
4 Beau - ti - ful Sav - ior, Lord of the na - tions,

Son of God and Son of Man!
Robed in flow'rs of bloom - ing spring;
Bright the spar - kling stars on high;
Son of God and Son of Man!

Tru - ly I'd love Thee, Tru - ly I'd serve Thee,
Je - sus is fair - er, Je - sus is pur - er,
Je - sus shines bright - er, Je - sus shines pur - er
Glo - ry and hon - or, Praise, ad - o - ra - tion

Light of my soul, my joy, my crown.
He makes our sor - r'wing spir - it sing.
Than all the an - gels in the sky.
Now and for - ev - er - more be Thine!

Text: Gesangbuch, Münster, 1677; tr. Joseph A. Seiss, 1823-1904
*Tune: **Schönster Herr Jesu**, Silesian folk tune, 1842*

Behold, What Manner of Love

Be - hold what man - ner of love the Fa - ther has giv - en un - to us! Be - hold what man-ner of love the Fa - ther has giv - en un - to us!

That we should be called the chil - dren of God,

That we should be called the chil-dren of God.

72 Beloved, Let Us Love One Another

Be - lov-ed, let us love one an - oth-er. For love is of God, and ev- 'ry-one that lov-eth is born of God and know-eth God, He that lov-eth not, know-eth not God, for God is love. Be - lov-ed, let us love one an - oth-er.

Best of All Friends

1 Je - sus, my Lord, let me be near You;
2 All through the day, sis - ters and bro - thers,
3 Teach us to know see - ing from blind-ness,

by Your own word help me to hear You.
Yours we will be, car - ing for oth - ers,
help us to show ev - 'ry-where kind-ness.

Je - sus, my Lord, lead me to love You,
hear - ing Your words, learn - ing Your sto - ry,
Je - sus, our Lord, lead us and guide us,

noth - ing more dear, no one a - bove You.
bear - ing Your cross, shar - ing Your glo - ry.
best of all friends, al - ways be - side us.

Blest Are They

1 Blest are they, the poor in spir - it;
2 Blest are they, the low - ly ones;___
5 Blest are you who suf - fer hate,___

theirs is the king-dom of God.___
they shall in - her - it the earth.___
all___ be - cause___ of me. Re -

Blest___ are they,___ full___ of sor - row;
Blest___ are they who hun-ger and thirst;
joice and be glad,___ yours is the king - dom;

they shall be con - soled.___
they shall have their fill.___
shine for all to see.___

Refrain

Re - joice___ and be glad!___

Bless - ed are you, ho - ly are you. Re -

joice_____ and be glad!_____ Yours is the king-dom of

God!_____

3 Blest are they who show mer - cy;
4 Blest are they who seek peace;

mer - cy shall__ be theirs._____
they are the chil - dren of God._____

Blest are they, the pure__ of heart;____
Blest are they who suf - fer in faith; the

they_____ shall see God!____
glo - ry of God__ is theirs.____

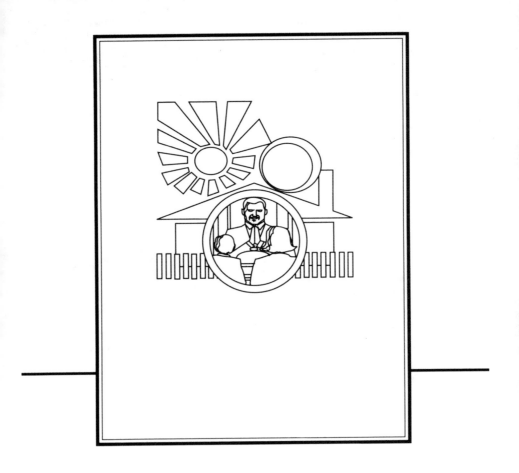

Blest the Children of Our God

75

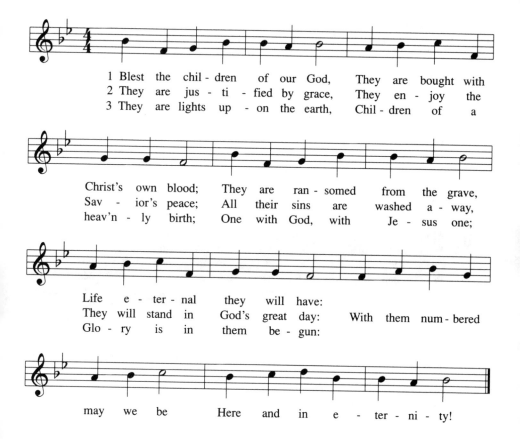

1 Blest the chil-dren of our God, They are bought with
2 They are jus-ti-fied by grace, They en-joy the
3 They are lights up-on the earth, Chil-dren of a

Christ's own blood; They are ran-somed from the grave,
Sav-ior's peace; All their sins are washed a-way,
heav'n-ly birth; One with God, with Je-sus one;

Life e-ter-nal they will have:
They will stand in God's great day: With them num-bered
Glo-ry is in them be-gun:

may we be Here and in e-ter-ni-ty!

Text: Joseph Humphreys, b. 1720, alt.
Tune: **Voller Wunder**, *Johann G. Ebeling, 1637-76*

76   Books of the Old Testament

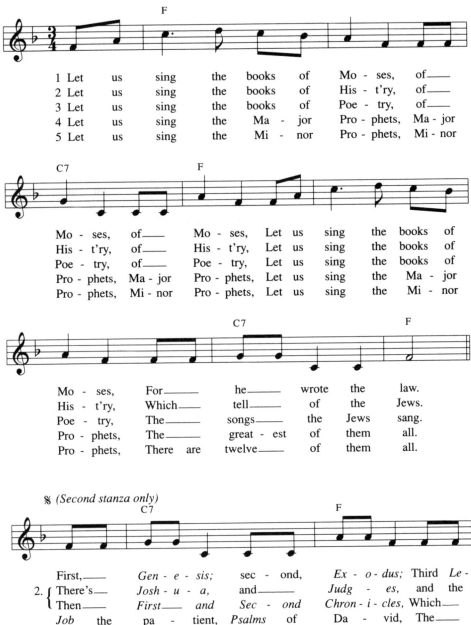

1 Let us sing the books of Mo - ses, of —
2 Let us sing the books of His - t'ry, of —
3 Let us sing the books of Poe - try, of —
4 Let us sing the Ma - jor Pro - phets, Ma - jor
5 Let us sing the Mi - nor Pro - phets, Mi - nor

Mo - ses, of — Mo - ses, Let us sing the books of
His - t'ry, of — His - t'ry, Let us sing the books of
Poe - try, of — Poe - try, Let us sing the books of
Pro - phets, Ma - jor Pro - phets, Let us sing the Ma - jor
Pro - phets, Mi - nor Pro - phets, Let us sing the Mi - nor

Mo - ses, For — he — wrote the law.
His - t'ry, Which — tell — of the Jews.
Poe - try, The — songs — the Jews sang.
Pro - phets, The — great - est of them all.
Pro - phets, There are twelve — of them all.

℀ (Second stanza only)

First, — Gen - e - sis; sec - ond, Ex - o - dus; Third Le -
2. { There's — Josh - u - a, and — Judg - es, and the
{ Then — First — and Sec - ond Chron - i - cles, Which —
Job the pa - tient, Psalms of Da - vid, The —
I - sai - ah, Jer - e - mi - ah, Who —
Hos - e - a, Joel, A - mos, O - ba - diah, Jo - nah,

vit - i - cus; Fourth__ Num-bers; And the fifth is Deu-ter-
sto - ry of__ Ruth__ Then__ First and Sec-ond
give__ us the__ Re-cords Then__ Ez - ra, Ne - he-
Pro - verbs of a wise one; And__ then Ec-cles-i-
wrote__ Lam - en - ta-tions; Then E - ze - kiel and__
Mi - cah, Na - hum, Ha - bak - kuk Zeph-a - ni - ah, Hag -

(Second stanza only)

on - o - my, The__ last of them__ all.
Sam - u - el, And__ First and Sec - ond Kings.
mi - ah, And__ Es - ther, the__ Queen.
as - tes, And the Song of Sol - o - mon.
Dan - iel, Who were true to their__ God.
ga - i, Zech - a - ri - ah, Mal - a - chi.

Text: arr. by I. M Tabor
Tune: unknown

77 Breath of the Living God

1 Breath of the liv - ing God on the wa - ters
2 Breath of the liv - ing God, You con - ceived the
3 Breath of the liv - ing God, You bring us to

in the be - gin - ning mov - ing,
Son, Je - sus, to be like us,
life in bap - tis - mal wa - ter,

Breath of the liv - ing God, You fill all cre -
Breath of the liv - ing God, so You re - cre -
Breath of the liv - ing God, we new crea - tures

a - tion with fruit - ful life.
ate all who live in Him.
live by Your liv - ing breath.

Refrain

Come now and live with - in us, and with Your gifts en - rich us:

Breath of the liv-ing God, O most ho-ly Spir-it— of the Lord!

1 Soplo de Dios viviente que en
el principio cubriste el agua;
Soplo de Dios viviente que
fecundaste la creación.
¡Ven hoy a nuestras almas,
infúndenos tus dones,
Soplo de Dios viviente,
oh Santo Espíritu del Señor!

2 Soplo de Dios viviente por
quien el hijo se hizo hombre,
Soplo de Dios viviente que
renovaste la creación.
¡Ven hoy a nuestras almas,
infúndenos tus dones,
Soplo de Dios viviente,
oh Santo Espíritu del Señor!

3 Soplo de Dios viviente por
quien nacemos en el bautismo;
Soplo de Dios viviente que
consagraste la creación.
¡Ven hoy a nuestras almas,
infúndenos tus dones,
Soplo de Dios viviente,
oh Santo Espíritu del Señor!

©Text: Osvaldo Catena; tr. Jaroslav Vajda, b. 1919
©Tune: Norwegian melody

Brothers and Sisters in Christ

1 Sing Al - le - lu - ia! A - men! Let your prayers and your
2 Man walked a - lone and in need, With-out faith, hope or
3 Lord, teach us how to pro - claim All Your good-ness, Your

prais - es as - cend. Lift up your voic - es and
prom - ise or creed; Wan - der - ing aim - less - ly
love and Your name! Lord, teach us how to for -

sing to our Lord God, our Sav - ior and King!
lost un - a - ware of the stag - ger-ing cost;
give, and in love, teach us Lord, how to live.

Here brought to - geth-er by grace, We are
That God in His mer-cy would save All His
Rais - ing our voic-es in song, Help us

gath-ered as friends in this place. And as - sem-bled as
peo - ple from death and the grave.
tell all the world we be - long.

one, in the name of the Son, Lift-ing hearts, lift-ing hands, Cel-e-

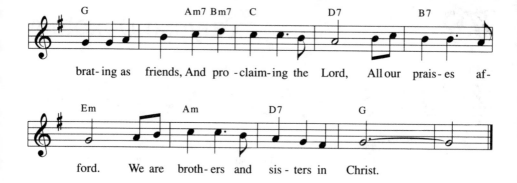

brat- ing as friends, And pro -claim- ing the Lord, All our prais- es af-

ford. We are broth- ers and sis - ters in Christ.

79

Calypso Doxology

1 Praise God from whom all bless-ings flow,— praise— Him
2 Hal - le - lu - jah! Got the vic - to - ry—

all ye crea - tures— here be - low.
o - ver Sa - tan and o - ver sin.

Praise Him a - bove, ye— heav'n - ly host, praise Him
Je - sus Christ is a - live to - day and He

Final Ending

Fa - ther, Son, and Ho - ly Ghost.
leads and guides me all the way.

Children of the Heavenly Father 80

1 Chil - dren of the heav'n - ly Fa - ther Safe - ly
2 God His own doth tend and nour - ish; In His
3 Nei - ther life nor death shall ev - er From the
4 Tho' He giv - eth or He tak - eth, God His

in His bos - om gath - er; Nest - ling bird nor star in
ho - ly courts they flour - ish. From all e - vil things He
Lord His chil - dren sev - er; Un - to them His grace He
chil - dren ne'er for - sak - eth. His the lov - ing pur - pose

heav - en Such a ref - uge e'er was giv - en.
spares them, In His might - y arms He bears them.
show - eth, And their sor - rows all He know - eth.
sole - ly To pre - serve them pure and ho - ly.

© *Text: Caroline V. Sandell Berg, 1832-1903; tr. Ernst William Olson, 1870-1958*
Tune: **Tryggare Kan ingen vara**, *Swedish folk tune*

81   Christ Be My Leader

1 Christ be my lead - er by night as by day;
Safe through the dark - ness, for He is the way._____
Glad - ly I fol - low, my fu - ture His care;_____
Dark-ness is day- light when Je - sus is there.

2 Christ be my teach - er in age as in youth,
Drift - ing or doubt - ing, for He is the truth._____
Grant me to trust Him; though shift - ing as sand,_____
Doubt can - not daunt me; in Je - sus I stand.

3 Christ be my sav - ior in calm as in strife;
Death can - not hold me, for He is the life.
Nor dark - ness nor doubt - ing nor sin and its stain
Can touch my sal - va - tion: with Je - sus I reign.

© Text: Timothy Dudley-Smith, b. 1926
Tune: **Slane**, Irish folk tune

Christ, the Life of All the Living 82

1 Christ, the Life of all the liv-ing, Christ, the death of
2 You have suf-fered great af-flic-tion And have borne it
3 Then, for all that bought my par-don, For the sor-rows

death, our foe, Christ, Your-self for me once giv-ing
pa - tient - ly, E - ven death by cru - ci - fix - ion,
deep and sore, For the an - guish in the gar - den,

To the dark - est depths of woe: Thro' Your suf - f'ring,
Ful - ly to a - tone for me; For You chose to
I will thank You ev - er-more, Thank You for the

death, and mer - it Life e - ter - nal I in - her - it.
be tor - ment - ed That my doom should be pre-vent - ed.
groan - ing, sigh - ing, For the bleed - ing and the dy - ing,

Thou-sand, thou-sand thanks are due, Dear - est Je-sus, un-to You.
Thou-sand, thou-sand thanks are due, Dear - est Je-sus, un-to You.
For that last tri - um - phant cry, Praise You ev - er - more on high.

Text: Ernst C. Homburg, 1605-81; tr. Catherine Winkworth 1829-78, alt.
*Tune: **Jesu, meines Lebens Leben,** Kirchengesangbuch, Darmstadt, 1687*

83 Christ the Lord Is Risen Today

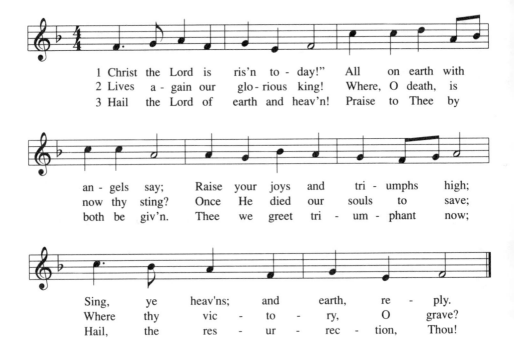

1 Christ the Lord is ris'n to - day!" All on earth with
2 Lives a - gain our glo - rious king! Where, O death, is
3 Hail the Lord of earth and heav'n! Praise to Thee by

an - gels say; Raise your joys and tri - umphs high;
now thy sting? Once He died our souls to save;
both be giv'n. Thee we greet tri - um - phant now;

Sing, ye heav'ns; and earth, re - ply.
Where thy vic - to - ry, O grave?
Hail, the res - ur - rec - tion, Thou!

Text: Charles Wesley, 1707-88, alt.
*Tune: **Orientis partibus**, French, 13th cent.*

84

Circle of Friends

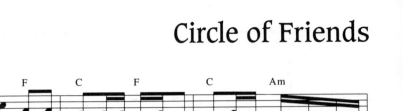

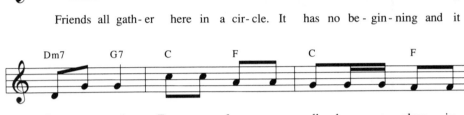

Friends all gath-er here in a cir-cle. It has no be-gin-ning and it

has no end. Face to face, we all have a place in

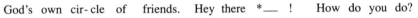

God's own cir-cle of friends. Hey there *___ ! How do you do?

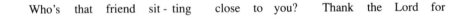

Who's that friend sit-ting close to you? Thank the Lord for

*___ has a place in the cir-cle too. Take a look a-round. Find

some-one near. Take him by the hand, say "Glad you're here."
(her)

We're to-geth-er and when we've gone, God's love like a cir-cle rolls

on and on and on.

85

"Come, Follow Me,"
Said Christ the Lord

1 "Come, fol-low me," said Christ, the Lord, "All in my way a-
2 "I am the light; I light the way, A god-ly life dis-
3 "My heart is rich in low-li-ness; My soul with love is
4 "I teach you how to shun and flee What harms your soul's sal-

bid - ing; Your self-ish-ness throw o-ver-board, O-
play - ing; I help you walk as in the day; I
glow - ing; My lips the words of grace ex-press, Their
va - tion; Your heart from ev-'ry guile to free, From

bey My call and guid-ing. Oh, bear Your cross-es,
keep your feet from stray-ing. I am the way, and
tones all gen-tly flow-ing. My heart, my mind, my
sin and its temp-ta-tion. I am the ref-uge

and con-fide In My ex-am-ple as your guide.
well I show How you should jour-ney here be-low.
strength, my all To God I yield; on Him I call.
of the soul And lead you to your heav'n-ly goal."

5 Then let us follow Christ, our Lord,
  And take the cross appointed
  And, firmly clinging to His word,
  In suff'ring be undaunted.
  For those who bear the battle's strain
  The crown of heav'nly life obtain.

Text: Johann Scheffler, 1624-77; tr. Charles W. Schaeffer, 1813-96, alt.
Tune: **Machs mit mir, Gott,** *Bartholomäus Gesius, c. 1555-1613, adapt.*

Come, Let Us Worship

86

87 Crown Him with Many Crowns

1 Crown Him with man-y crowns, The Lamb up - on His
2 Crown Him the Lord of life, Who tri - umphed o'er the
3 Crown Him the Lord of heav'n, En - throned in worlds a -

throne; Hark how the heav'n - ly an - them drowns All
grave And rose vic - to - rious in the strife For
bove, Crown Him the king to whom is giv'n The

mu - sic but its own. A - wake, my soul, and
those He came to save. His glo - ries now we
won - drous name of Love. Crown Him with man - y

sing Of Him who died for thee, And
sing, Who died and rose on high, Who
crowns As thrones be - fore Him fall; Crown

hail Him as thy match - less king Through all e - ter - ni - ty.
died e - ter - nal life to bring And lives that death may die.
Him, ye kings, with man - y crowns, For He is king of all.

Text: Matthew Bridges, 1800-94; Godfrey Thring, 1823-1903, alt.
*Tune: **Diademata**, George J. Elvey, 1816-93*

Dear Christians, One and All, Rejoice

88

1 Dear Chris - tians, one and all, now re - joice, With
2 God's Son o - beyed the heav - en - ly will When
3 All life and praise and hon - or shall be To

ex - ul - ta - tion spring - ing, And with u - nit - ed
born of vir - gin moth - er. He came to live, to
Fa - ther, Son, and Spir - it. Thank Him who made our

heart, mind, and voice And ho - ly rap - ture sing - ing, Pro -
love and ful - fill, To be our Friend and Broth - er. From
sal - va - tion free, And joy-ful - ly go share it! Oh,

claim the won-ders our God has done, E - ter - nal life for
sin and sor - row we now are free, Sal - va - tion sent that
tri - une God in heav - en a - bove, Who of - fers all His

us is won; Se - vere - ly it has cost Him.
we may be In Par - a - dise for - ev - er.
sav - ing love, Your name be praised un - end - ing!

Text: Martin Luther, 1483-1546; tr. Richard Massie, 1800-87, alt.
*Tune: **Nun freut euch,** Etlich' Christliche lider, Wittenberg, 1524, alt.*

89 Do Lord!: Psalm 27

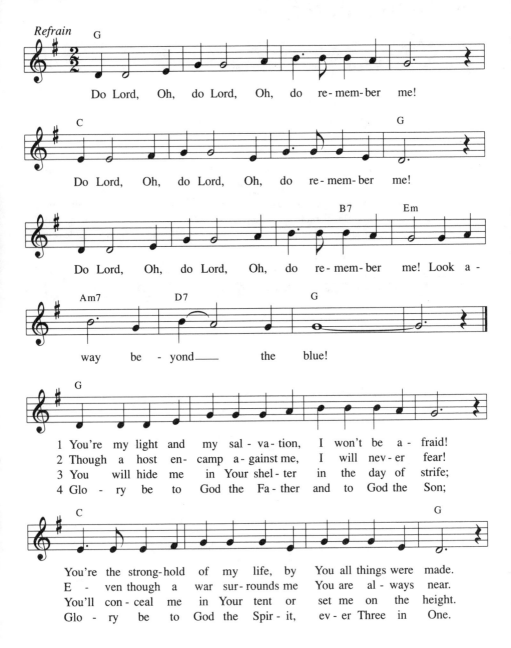

Refrain

Do Lord, Oh, do Lord, Oh, do re-mem-ber me!

Do Lord, Oh, do Lord, Oh, do re-mem-ber me!

Do Lord, Oh, do Lord, Oh, do re-mem-ber me! Look a-

way be-yond___ the blue!

1 You're my light and my sal-va-tion, I won't be a-fraid!
2 Though a host en-camp a-gainst me, I will nev-er fear!
3 You will hide me in Your shel-ter in the day of strife;
4 Glo-ry be to God the Fa-ther and to God the Son;

You're the strong-hold of my life, by You all things were made.
E-ven though a war sur-rounds me You are al-ways near.
You'll con-ceal me in Your tent or set me on the height.
Glo-ry be to God the Spir-it, ev-er Three in One.

Foes at-tack me, has-sle me, but I will nev-er fade, For I
One thing I have asked of You that I will seek for sure Is to
Now my head is lift-ed up a - bove the storms of night, So I'll
As it was in the be-gin-ning till our race is won, We can

move in the strength of the Lord.
live in the house of the Lord.
sing to the name of the Lord.
live in the light of the Lord.

90 Earth and All Stars

1 Earth and all stars! Loud rush-ing plan - ets!
2 Hail, wind, and rain! Loud blow-ing snow - storm!
3 Trum - pet and pipes! Loud clash-ing cym - bals!
4 En - gines and steel! Loud pound-ing ham - mers!

Sing to the Lord_____ a new song!
Sing to the Lord_____ a new song!
Sing to the Lord_____ a new song!
Sing to the Lord_____ a new song!

Oh, vic - to - ry! Loud shout - ing ar - my!
Flow - ers and trees! Loud rus - tling dry leaves!
Harp, lute, and lyre! Loud hum - ming cel - los!
Lime - stone and beams! Loud build - ing work - ers!

Sing to the Lord_____ a new song!
Sing to the Lord_____ a new song!
Sing to the Lord_____ a new song!
Sing to the Lord_____ a new song!

Refrain

He has done mar - velous things.

I too will praise Him with a new song!

5 Classrooms and labs!
  Loud boiling test tubes!
  Sing to the Lord a new song!
  Athlete and band!
  Loud cheering people!
  Sing to the Lord a new song! *Refrain*

6 Knowledge and truth!
  Loud sounding wisdom!
  Sing to the Lord a new song!
  Daughter and son!
  Loud praying members!
  Sing to the Lord a new song! *Refrain*

7 Children of God,
  Dying and rising,
  Sing to the Lord a new song!
  Heaven and earth,
  Hosts everlasting,
  Sing to the Lord a new song! *Refrain*

91

Easter Song

F C F C F C F C F

1 Hear the bells ring - ing, they're sing - ing that we can be
2 Hear the bells ring - ing, they're sing - ing, "Christ is ris - en

Bb F C C | 1 C

born a - gain! _____
from the dead!" _____

| 2 C Am C7/G F7 F

The an - gel up - on the tombstone said,

Am C7/G Am7/G F7 F Dm Dm7/C

"He is ris - en just as He said, Quick - ly now go

Bb7 Bb Am C7/G Am7/G F7 F

tell His dis - ci - ples that Je - sus Christ is no long - er

C/E Dm Dm/C Bb F

dead!" Joy to the world, He is ris - en, Al -

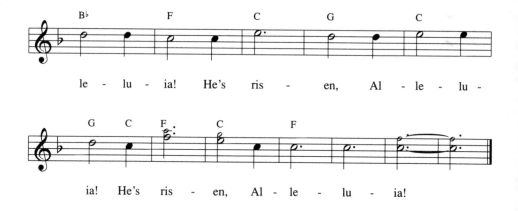

le - lu - ia! He's ris - en, Al - le - lu -

ia! He's ris - en, Al - le - lu - ia!

92

El Shaddai

El Shad-dai, El Shad-dai, El El - yon na A - do-nai;

—— age to age You're still the same by the pow-er of the name.

—— El Shad-dai, El Shad-dai, Er-kahm - ka na A - do- nai;

—— we will praise and lift You high, El Shad - dai.

Every Time I Feel the Spirit

Ev - 'ry time I feel the spir - it, mov - ing
in my heart, I will pray.____ Ev - 'ry - time I feel the
spir - it, mov - ing in my heart, I will pray.

Up - on the moun - tain my Lord spoke,
All a - round me looked so shine,
Jor - dan riv - er, chilly and cold,

D.C.

(Out of) his mouth came____ fire and smoke.
Asked____ my Lord if all was mine.
Chills the bod - y but not the soul.

94

Father, I Adore You

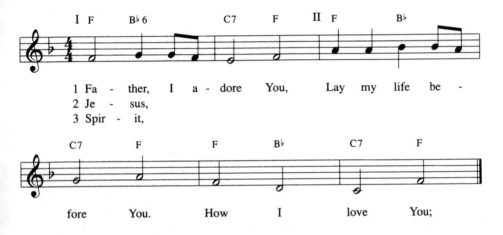

1 Fa - ther, I a - dore You, Lay my life be -
2 Je - sus,
3 Spir - it,

fore You. How I love You;

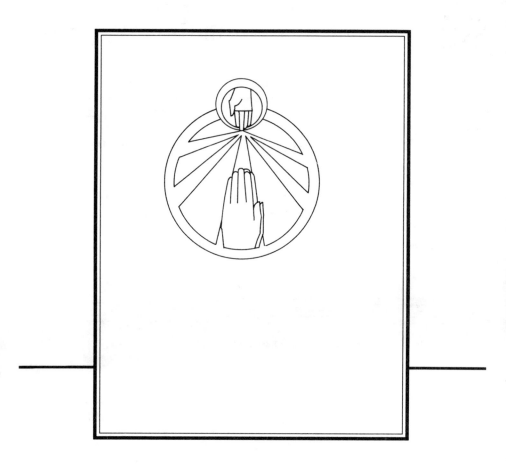

95   Father Welcomes

Fa - ther wel-comes all His chil-dren to His fam-'ly
through His Son. Fa - ther giv-ing His sal - va-tion,
Life for - ev - er has been won.   won.

1 Lit - tle chil - dren, come to me,
2 In the wa - ter, in the Word,
3 Let us dai - ly die to sin;

for My king - dom is of these.
in His prom - ise, be as - sured:
let us dai - ly rise with Him

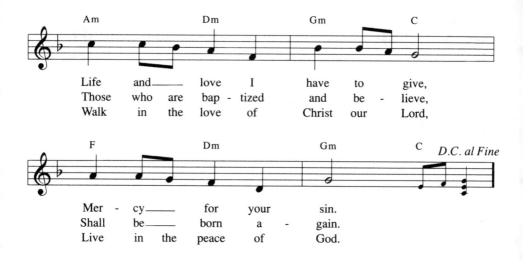

Life and love I have to give,
Those who are bap - tized and be - lieve,
Walk in the love of Christ our Lord,

Mer - cy for your sin.
Shall be born a - gain.
Live in the peace of God.

©Text: Robin Mann
©Tune: Robin Mann

96   Forgive Our Sins as We Forgive

1 "For - give our sins   as   we for - give," You
2 How   can Your par - don   reach   and   bless   The
3 In   blaz - ing light   Your   cross   re - veals   The
4 Lord,   cleanse the depths   with - in   our   souls   And

taught us, Lord,   to   pray;   But   You   a - lone   can
un - for - giv - ing   heart   That   broods on   wrongs   and
truth   we   dim - ly   knew: How   tri - fling   oth - ers'
bid   re - sent - ment   cease;   Then,   by   Your   mer - cy

grant   us   grace   To   live   the words   we   say.
will   not   let   Old   bit - ter - ness   de - part?
debts   to   us;   How   great   our debt   to   You!
rec - on - ciled,   Our   lives   will spread   Your   peace.

© Text: Rosamond E. Herklots, 1905-87, alt.
Tune: **Detroit,** The Sacred Harp, Philadephia, 1844

Forgive Us, Lord, for Shallow Thankfulness

1 For-give us, Lord, for shal-low thank-ful-ness, For
2 Teach us to thank You, Lord, for love and grace, For
3 For-give us, Lord, for self-ish thanks and praise, For
4 Teach us, O Lord, true thank-ful-ness di-vine, That

dull con-tent with warmth and shel-tered care, For
life and vi-sion, for a pur-pose clear, For
words that speak at var-i-ance with deeds; Forgives as Christ gave, nev-er count-ing cost, That

songs of praise for world-ly wealth-i-ness, While
Christ Your Son, and for each hu-man face That
give our thanks for walk-ing pleas-ant ways Un-
knows no bar-ri-er of "yours" and "mine," As-

of Your rich-er gifts we're un-a-ware:
shows Your mes-sage ev-er new and near.
mind-ful of a bro-ken broth-er's needs:
sured that on-ly what's with-held is lost.

5 Forgive us, Lord, for feast that knows not fast,
For joy in things that meanwhile starve the soul,
For walls and wars that hide Your mercies vast
And blur our vision of the Kingdom goal:

6 Open our eyes to see Your love's intent,
To know with minds and hearts its depth and height;
Let thankful days in loving labor spent
Reflect the truly Christ-like life and light.

©Text: William W. Reid Sr., 1890-1983, alt.
©Tune: **Sursum corda**, Alfred M. Smith, 1879-1971

98

From Heaven Above
to Earth I Come

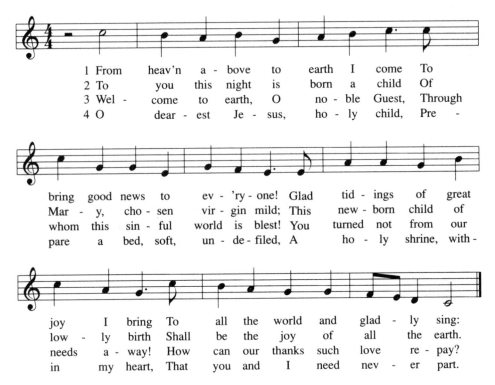

1 From heav'n a - bove to earth I come To
2 To you this night is born a child Of
3 Wel - come to earth, O no - ble Guest, Through
4 O dear - est Je - sus, ho - ly child, Pre -

bring good news to ev - 'ry - one! Glad tid - ings of great
Mar - y, cho - sen vir - gin mild; This new - born child of
whom this sin - ful world is blest! You turned not from our
pare a bed, soft, un - de - filed, A ho - ly shrine, with -

joy I bring To all the world and glad - ly sing:
low - ly birth Shall be the joy of all the earth.
needs a - way! How can our thanks such love re - pay?
in my heart, That you and I need nev - er part.

©*Text: Martin Luther, 1483-1546;* Lutheran Book of Worship, *1978*
Tune: **Vom Himmel hoch,** *Valentin Schumann,* Geistliche Lieder, *Leipzig, 1539*

"Glory Be to God on High"

1 "Glo-ry be to God on high!"— This is now our joy-ful cry.
2 Je - sus Christ, the Fath-er's Son,— Sole-be-got - ten, ho - ly One,

Peace to all who live on earth,— Grace and fa - vor for new birth.
Born on earth from realms on high,— Born true man for us to die,

You we praise and glo-ri-fy,— Wor - ship You, O Lord most high.—
Lamb of God, You take a-way— This world's sin: Grant peace we pray.—

Gra-cious Fa-ther, heav'n - ly King, To Your name a - lone we sing:
With the Spir-it, You a-lone Are most high, O God the Son,

Praise the glo-ry of Your name, Now and ev - er - more the same!
And the Fa-ther, God a - bove. Praise we now Your glo-rious love.

© Text: Bradford Scott
Tune: **Mendelssohn**, Felix Mendelssohn, 1809-47

100 Glory to God in the Highest

Glory to God in the highest, and peace to His peo-ple on earth.

Lord God, heav-en-ly king, al-might-y God and Fa - ther

We wor - ship You, we give You thanks,

we praise You for Your glo - ry.

Lord Je - sus Christ, on - ly Son of the Fa - ther,

Lord God, Lamb of God: You take a-way the sin of the world;

have mer - cy on us.

You are seat - ed at the right hand of the Fa - ther;

re - ceive   our   prayer.

For You a - lone   are the Ho - ly One,

You a- lone are the Lord,   You a- lone are the Most High,

Je - sus Christ,   with the Ho - ly Spir - it,

in the glo - ry   of God the Fa - ther A - men.

©Text: International Consultation on English Texts
©Tune: Richard W. Hillert, b. 1923

101   Go into the World

Go ye, go ye in- to the world and make dis- ci - ples of all the na tions,

Go ye, go ye in- to the world and I will be with you there!

I am the vine, you are the branch - es, ev - er the fruit to bear;

I am the light, you, the re- flec- tion ev - 'ry - where.

Go, My Children, with My Blessing

1 Go, My chil-dren, with My bless-ing, nev-er a-
2 Go, My chil-dren, sins for-giv-en, at peace and
3 Go, My chil-dren, fed and nour-ished, clos-er to
4 I the Lord will bless and keep you and give you

lone; Wak-ing, sleep-ing, I am with you,
pure. Here you learned how much I love you,
Me; Grow in love and love by serv-ing,
peace. I the Lord will smile up-on you

you are My own. In My love's bap-
what I can cure. Here you heard My
joy-ful and free. Here My Spir-it's
and give you peace. I the Lord will

tis-mal riv-er I have made you Mine for-ev-er.
dear Son's sto-ry, Here you touched Him, saw His glo-ry.
pow-er filled you, here His ten-der com-fort stilled you.
be your Fa-ther, Sav-ior, Com-fort-er and Broth-er.

Go, My chil-dren, with My bless-ing, you are My own.
Go, My chil-dren, sins for-giv-en, at peace and pure.
Go, My chil-dren, fed and nour-ished, joy-ful and free.
Go, My chil-dren, I will keep you and give you peace.

© Text: Jaroslav J. Vajda, b. 1919
Tune: **Ar hyd y nos**, Welsh

103

Go Now in Peace

Keyboard, handbells, *and/or Orff instruments*

I Go now in peace,

II go now in peace, may the love of God sur - round you

III ev - 'ry - where, ev - 'ry - where you may go.

Fine

May be sung as a canon

Go Tell It on the Mountain 104

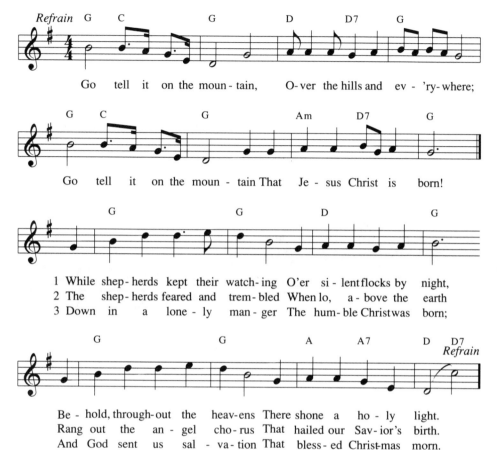

Refrain

Go tell it on the moun-tain, O-ver the hills and ev-'ry-where;

Go tell it on the moun-tain That Je - sus Christ is born!

1 While shep-herds kept their watch-ing O'er si - lent flocks by night,
2 The shep-herds feared and trem-bled When lo, a-bove the earth
3 Down in a lone-ly man-ger The hum-ble Christ was born;

Be - hold, through-out the heav-ens There shone a ho - ly light.
Rang out the an - gel cho-rus That hailed our Sav-ior's birth.
And God sent us sal - va-tion That bless-ed Christ-mas morn.

105   Go to Dark Gethsemane

1 Go to dark Geth - sem - a - ne, All who feel the
2 Fol - low to the judg- ment hall, View the Lord of
3 Cal - v'ry's mourn - ful moun- tain climb; There, a - dor - ing
4 Ear - ly has - ten to the tomb Where they laid His

tempt - er's pow'r; Your Re - deem - er's con - flict see.
life ar - raigned; Oh, the worm - wood and the gall!
at His feet, Mark that mir - a - cle of time,
breath- less clay; All is sol - i - tude and gloom.

Watch with Him one bit - ter hour; Turn not from His
Oh, the pangs His soul sus - tained! Shun not suf - f'ring,
God's own sac - ri - fice com - plete. "It is fin - ished!"
Who has tak - en Him a - way? Christ is ris'n! He

griefs a - way; Learn from Je - sus Christ to pray.
shame, or loss; Learn from Him to bear the cross.
hear Him cry; Learn from Je - sus Christ to die.
meets our eyes. Sav - ior, teach us so to rise.

Text: James Montgomery, 1771-1854
Tune: **Gethsemane**, *Richard Redhead, 1820-1901*

God Bless Our Native Land

106

1 God bless our na-tive land; Firm may it ev-er stand
2 So shall our prayers a-rise To God a-bove the skies,

Through storm and night. When the wild
On whom we wait. Thou who art

tem-pests rave, Rul-er of wind and wave,
ev-er nigh, Guard-ing with watch-ful eye,

Do Thou our coun-try save By Thy great might.
To Thee a-loud we cry: God save the state!

Text: tr. Charles Timothy Brooks, 1812-83, st. 1; John Sullivan Dwight, 1813-93, st. 2, alt.
*Tune: **National Anthem**, Thesaurus Musicus, England, 1740*

107

God Is So Good

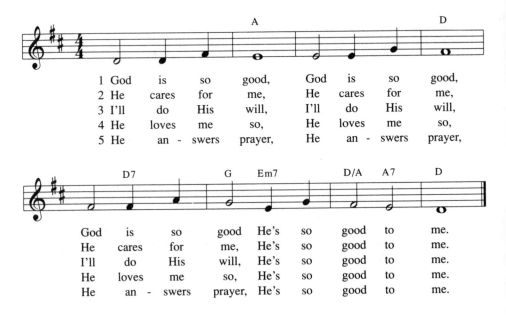

1 God is so good, God is so good,
2 He cares for me, He cares for me,
3 I'll do His will, I'll do His will,
4 He loves me so, He loves me so,
5 He an - swers prayer, He an - swers prayer,

God is so good He's so good to me.
He cares for me, He's so good to me.
I'll do His will, He's so good to me.
He loves me so, He's so good to me.
He an - swers prayer, He's so good to me.

Text: author unknown
Tune: African melody

God Loved the World So that He Gave   108

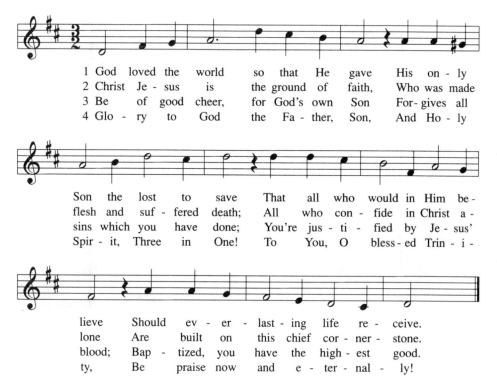

1 God loved the world so that He gave His on - ly
2 Christ Je - sus is the ground of faith, Who was made
3 Be of good cheer, for God's own Son For - gives all
4 Glo - ry to God the Fa - ther, Son, And Ho - ly

Son the lost to save That all who would in Him be -
flesh and suf - fered death; All who con - fide in Christ a -
sins which you have done; You're jus - ti - fied by Je - sus'
Spir - it, Three in One! To You, O bless - ed Trin - i -

lieve Should ev - er - last - ing life re - ceive.
lone Are built on this chief cor - ner - stone.
blood; Bap - tized, you have the high - est good.
ty, Be praise now and e - ter - nal - ly!

Text: L. Bollhagen, Heiliges Lippen- und Herzens-Opfer, c. 1778; tr. August
    Crull, 1845-1923, alt.
Tune: **Die helle Sonn leucht,** Melchior Vulpius, c. 1560-1615

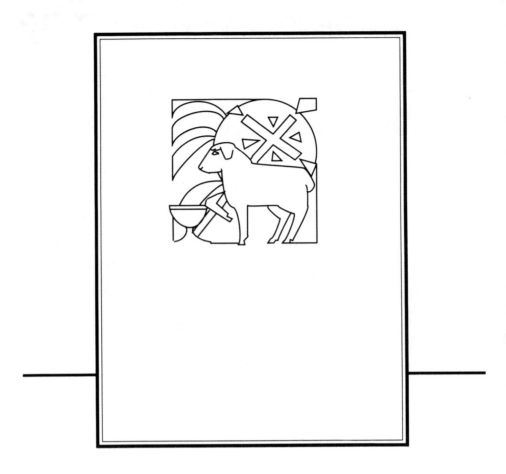

God Loves Me Dearly

1 God loves me dear - ly, Grants me sal -
2 I was in slav - 'ry, Sin, death, and
3 He sent forth Je - sus, My dear Re -
4 Je - sus, my Sav - ior, Him - self did

va - tion, God loves me dear - ly, Loves e - ven me.
dark - ness; God's love was work - ing To make me free.
deem - er, He sent forth Je - sus And set me free.
of - fer; Je - sus, my Sav - ior, Paid all I owed.

Refrain

There - fore I'll say a - gain: God loves me

dear - ly, God loves me dear - ly, Loves e - ven me.

5 Now I will praise You,
   O Love Eternal;
   Now I will praise You
   All my life long. *Refrain*

Text: August Rische 19th cent.; tr. composite
Tune: **Gott ist die Liebe,** *German folk tune*

110 God of Grace and God of Glory

1 God of grace and God of glo - ry,
2 Lo, the hosts of e - vil round us
3 Cure Your chil - dren's war - ring mad - ness;
4 Save us from weak res - ig - na - tion

On Your peo - ple pour Your pow'r;
Scorn the Christ, as - sail His ways!
Bend our pride to Your con - trol;
To the e - vils we de - plore;

Crown Your an - cient church's sto - ry;
From the fears that long have bound us
Shame our wan - ton, self - ish glad - ness,
Let the gift of Your sal - va - tion

Bring its bud to glo - rious flow'r.
Free our hearts to faith and praise.
Rich in things and poor in soul.
Be our glo - ry ev - er - more.

Grant us wis - dom, grant us cour - age
Grant us wis - dom, grant us cour - age
Grant us wis - dom, grant us cour - age
Grant us wis - dom, grant us cour - age,

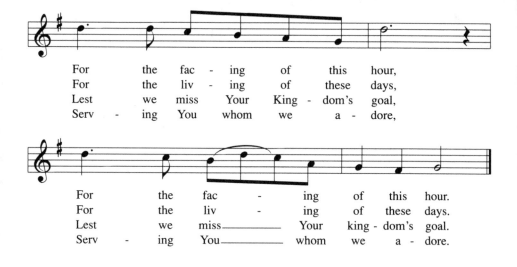

For   the   fac - ing   of   this   hour,
For   the   liv - ing   of   these   days,
Lest   we   miss   Your   King - dom's   goal,
Serv - ing   You   whom   we   a - dore,

For   the   fac - ing   of   this   hour.
For   the   liv - ing   of   these   days.
Lest   we   miss——— Your   king - dom's   goal.
Serv - ing   You——— whom   we   a - dore.

Text: Harry E. Fosdick, 1878-1969
*Tune: **Cwm Rhondda**, John Hughes, 1873-1932*

111 God of the Sparrow

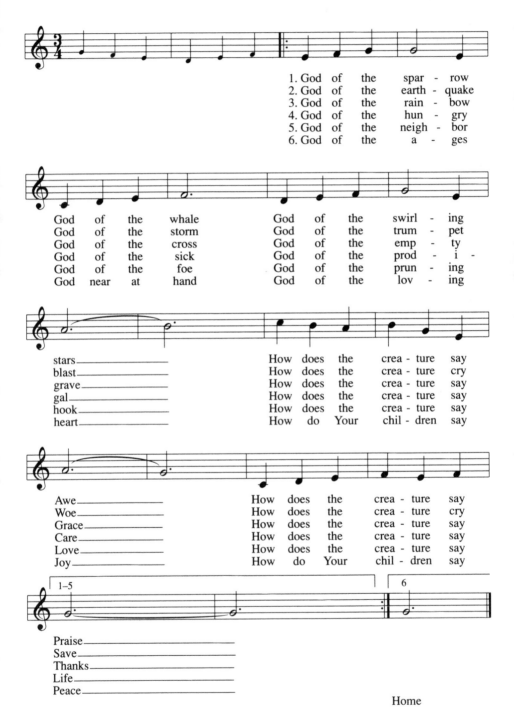

1. God of the spar - row
2. God of the earth - quake
3. God of the rain - bow
4. God of the hun - gry
5. God of the neigh - bor
6. God of the a - ges

God of the whale   God of the swirl - ing
God of the storm   God of the trum - pet
God of the cross   God of the emp - ty
God of the sick   God of the prod - i -
God of the foe   God of the prun - ing
God near at hand   God of the lov - ing

stars   How does the crea - ture say
blast   How does the crea - ture cry
grave   How does the crea - ture say
gal   How does the crea - ture say
hook   How does the crea - ture say
heart   How do Your chil - dren say

Awe   How does the crea - ture say
Woe   How does the crea - ture cry
Grace   How does the crea - ture say
Care   How does the crea - ture say
Love   How does the crea - ture say
Joy   How do Your chil - dren say

1–5   6

Praise
Save
Thanks
Life
Peace

Home

© Text: Jaroslav J. Vajda, b.1919
© Tune: **Roeder**, Carl F. Schalk, b. 1929

Good Christian Friends, Rejoice and Sing

112

1 Good Chris - tian friends, re - joice and
2 The Lord of life is ris'n this
3 Praise we in songs of vic - to -
4 Your name we bless, O ris - en

sing! Now is the tri - umph of our
day; Bring flow'rs of song to strew His
ry That love, that life which can - not
Lord, And sing to - day with one ac -

King! To all the world glad news we bring:
way; Let all the world re - joice and say:
die, And sing with hearts up - lift - ed high:
cord The life laid down, the life re - stored:

Al - le - lu - ia,_____ al - le - lu - ia,_____ al - le - lu - ia!

©Text: Cyril A. Alington, 1872-1955, alt.
Tune: **Gelobt sei Gott**, Melchior Vulpius, c. 1570-1615

113 Hail Thee, Festival Day

Refrain

Hail thee, fes - ti- val day! Blest day to be hal - lowed for - ev - er;

1st time | *2nd time*

Day when our Lord was raised, break-ing the king- dom of death. death.

Stanzas 1, 3, 5

1 All the fair beau - ty of earth from
3 God the Al - might - y, the Lord, the
5 Spir - it of life and of pow'r, now

death of the win - ter a - ris - ing! Ev - 'ry good
rul - er of earth and the heav - ens, Guard us from
flow in us, fount of our be - ing, Light that en -

Repeat refrain once after each stanza

gift of the year___ now with its mas - ter re - turns:
harm with - out;___ cleanse us from e - vil with - in:
light - ens us all,___ life that in all may a - bide:

Stanzas 2, 4, 6

2 Rise from the grave now, O Lord, the au - thor of
4 Je - sus, the health of the world, en - light - en our
6 Praise to the giv - er of good! O Lov - er and

life and cre - a - tion. Tread-ing the path-way of
minds, great re - deem - er, Son of the Fa - ther su -
Au - thor of con - cord, Pour out Your balm on our

death, new life You give to us all:_____
preme, on - ly - be - got - ten of God:_____
days; or - der our ways in Your peace:_____

©*Text: Venantius Honorius Fortunatus, 530-609; tr.* Lutheran Book of
Worship, *1978*
Tune: **Salve festa dies**, *Ralph Vaughan Williams, 1872-1958*

114 Hallelujah! Praise Ye the Lord!

Hal-le - lu! Hal-le-lu! Hal-le-lu! Hal-le-lu-jah! Praise ye the Lord!

Hal-le -lu! Hal-le-lu! Hal-le-lu! Hal-le-lu-jah! Praise ye the Lord!

Praise ye the Lord! Hal-le-lu-jah! Praise ye the Lord! Hal-le-lu-jah!

Praise ye the Lord! Hal - le - lu - jah! Praise ye the Lord!

Text: traditional
*Tune: **Hallelujah!***

Have No Fear, Little Flock

115

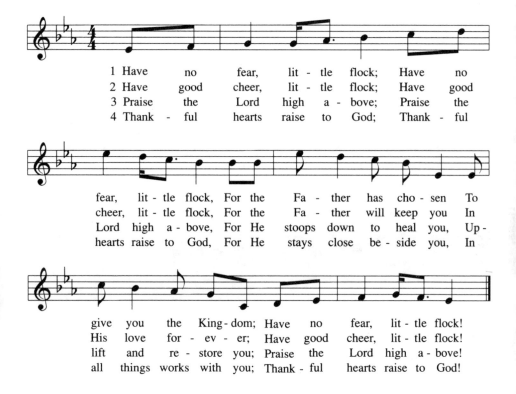

1 Have no fear, lit - tle flock; Have no
2 Have good cheer, lit - tle flock; Have good
3 Praise the Lord high a - bove; Praise the
4 Thank - ful hearts raise to God; Thank - ful

fear, lit - tle flock, For the Fa - ther has cho - sen To
cheer, lit - tle flock, For the Fa - ther will keep you In
Lord high a - bove, For He stoops down to heal you, Up -
hearts raise to God, For He stays close be - side you, In

give you the King - dom; Have no fear, lit - tle flock!
His love for - ev - er; Have good cheer, lit - tle flock!
lift and re - store you; Praise the Lord high a - bove!
all things works with you; Thank - ful hearts raise to God!

116 He Is Born, the Child Divine

1 Proph - ets from the___ a - ges past Have fore -
2 Ah! How fair is the Ho - ly Child, And how
3 In a man - ger___ was He born; Straw, a
4 King of all for - ev - er - more, Lit - tle

Loo,___

told the Sav - ior's com - ing; We for more than four
per - fect are His grac - es; Ah, how fair is the
lit - tle, for His cra - dle; In a man - ger
In - fant though Thou art, King of all for -

loo,___ loo,___

thou - sand years Have a - wait - ed this joy - ous time.
Ho - ly Child; Oh, how sweet is the Child Di - vine!
was He born, What a lodg - ing for Christ, the Lord!
ev - er - more, Reign in ev - 'ry hu - man heart.

Refrain

loo.___

Text: traditional
Tune: **Il est né le Divin Enfant,** *traditional French carol*

He's Got the Whole World in His Hands

1 He's got the whole_____ world___ in His hands, He's got the
2 He's got the wind___ and the rain___ in His hands, He's got the
3 He's got the ti - ny lit-tle ba - by in His hands, He's got the
4 He's got___ you and me,___ broth-er in His hands, He's got___

whole_ wide___ world___ in His hands, He's got the whole_____ world___
sun___ and the moon___ in His hands, He's got the wind___ and the rain___
ti - ny lit-tle ba - by in His hands, He's got the ti - ny lit-tle ba - by
you and me,___ sis-ter, in His hands, He's got___ you and me,___ broth-er,

in His hands, He's got the whole world in His hands.
in His hands, He's got the whole world in His hands.
in His hands, He's got the whole world in His hands.
in His hands, He's got the whole world in His hands.

Text: American spiritual
*Tune: **In His Hands**, American spiritual*

118 His Banner over Me Is Love

F

me____	is	love.____
me____	is	love.____
me____	is	love.____
me____	is	love.____

5 He lifts me up to the heavenly places, His banner over me is love . . .

6 One way to peace through the power of the cross, His banner over me is love . . .

Text: Psalm 40:2; John 5:5; unknown
Tune: anonymous

119

Holy, Holy, Holy!

1 Ho - ly, ho - ly, ho - ly! Lord___ God Al - might - y!
2 Ho - ly, ho - ly, ho - ly! All the saints a - dore Thee,
3 Ho - ly, ho - ly, ho - ly! Though the dark - ness hide Thee,
4 Ho - ly, ho - ly, ho - ly! Lord___ God Al - might - y!

Ear - ly in the morn - ing our song shall rise to Thee.
Cast - ing down their gold - en crowns a - round the glass - y sea;
Though the eye made blind by sin Thy glo - ry may not see,
All Thy works shall praise Thy name in earth and sky and sea.

Ho - ly, ho - ly, ho - ly, mer - ci - ful and might - y!
Cher - u - bim and ser - a - phim fall - ing down be - fore Thee,
On - ly Thou art ho - ly; there is none be - side Thee,
Ho - ly, ho - ly, ho - ly, mer - ci - ful and might - y!

God in three Per - sons, bless - ed Trin - i - ty!
Which wert and art and ev - er - more shalt be.
Per - fect in pow'r, in love and pu - ri - ty.
God in three Per - sons, bless - ed Trin - i - ty!

Text: Reginald Heber, 1783-1826
*Tune: **Nicaea**, John B. Dykes, 1823-76*

Holy Spirit, Light Divine

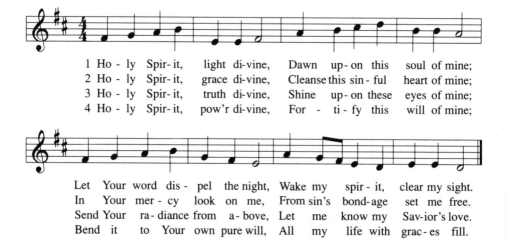

1 Ho - ly Spir- it,   light di-vine,   Dawn up- on this   soul of mine;
2 Ho - ly Spir- it,   grace di-vine,   Cleanse this sin - ful   heart of mine;
3 Ho - ly Spir- it,   truth di-vine,   Shine up- on these   eyes of mine;
4 Ho - ly Spir- it,   pow'r di-vine,   For - ti - fy this   will of mine;

Let Your word dis - pel the night,   Wake my spir - it,   clear my sight.
In Your mer - cy look on me,   From sin's bond-age   set me free.
Send Your ra- diance from a- bove,   Let me know my   Sav-ior's love.
Bend it to Your own pure will,   All my life with   grac- es fill.

5 Holy Spirit, peace divine,
  Still this restless heart of mine;
  Speak to calm the tossing sea,
  Stayed in Your tranquility.

6 Holy Spirit, all divine,
  Dwell within this self of mine;
  I Your temple pure would be
  Now and for eternity.

Text: Andrew Reed, 1788-1862, and Samuel Longfellow, 1819-92, alt.
Tune: **Song 13**, *Orlando Gibbons, 1583-1625*

121 Hosanna, Hallelujah

Refrain

Ho - san - na, hal - le - lu - jah! Sing we loud and clear. Ho - san - na, hal - le - lu - jah! Je - sus Christ is near. With an - cient psalms and new-grown palms Praise Him on His way. Ho - san - na, hal - le - lu - jah! Christ, our Lord, is here.

1 This day in spring the streets will ring with voic - es sweet and lyr - i - cal To greet our Lord, the One a - dored, His ver - y life a mir - a - cle.

2 King Da - vid's Son now rides up - on a mule, of beasts the low - li - est; A - midst the throng it bears a - long of all man - kind the ho - li - est.

3 How ver - y odd the Son of God must do things that would wear - y us. God will a - maze; He works in ways that we all find mys - te - ri - ous.

©Text: Richard K. Avery, b. 1934; Donald S. Marsh, b. 1923
©Tune: **Hosanna, Hallelujah!**, Richard K. Avery, b. 1934; Donald S. Marsh, 1923

How Majestic Is Your Name

122

O Lord, our Lord, how ma - jes - tic is Your name in all the earth. O Lord, our Lord, how ma - jes - tic is Your name in all the earth. O Lord, We praise Your name. O Lord, We mag - ni - fy Your name, Prince of Peace, might- y God, O Lord God Al - might - y.

123

How Precious Is the Book Divine

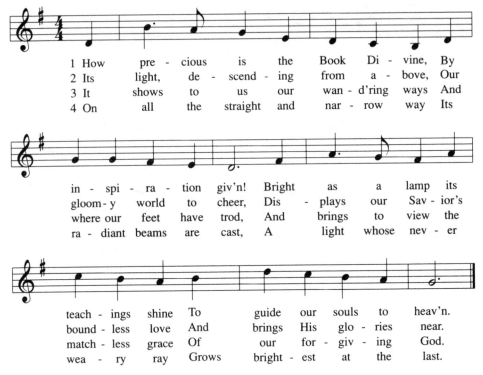

1 How pre - cious is the Book Di - vine, By
2 Its light, de - scend - ing from a - bove, Our
3 It shows to us our wan - d'ring ways And
4 On all the straight and nar - row way Its

in - spi - ra - tion giv'n! Bright as a lamp its
gloom - y world to cheer, Dis - plays our Sav - ior's
where our feet have trod, And brings to view the
ra - diant beams are cast, A light whose nev - er

teach - ings shine To guide our souls to heav'n.
bound - less love And brings His glo - ries near.
match - less grace Of our for - giv - ing God.
wea - ry ray Grows bright - est at the last.

Text: John Fawcett, 1749-1817, alt.
*Tune: **Walder**, Johann Jakob Walder, 1750-1817*

I Am a "C"

Text: unknown
Tune: unknown

125   I Am Jesus' Little Lamb

1 I am Je - sus' lit - tle lamb, Ev - er
2 Day by day, at home, a - way, Je - sus
3 Who so hap - py as I am, E - ven

glad at heart I am; For my Shep - herd gent - ly
is my staff and stay. When I hun - ger, Je - sus
now the Shep - herd's lamb? And when my short life is

guides me, Knows my need and well pro - vides me, Loves me
feeds me, In - to pleas - ant pas - tures leads me; When I
end - ed, By His an - gel host at - tend - ed, He shall

ev - 'ry day the same, E - ven calls me by my name.
thirst, He bids me go Where the qui - et wa - ters flow.
fold me to His breast, There with - in His arms to rest.

Text: Henrietta L. von Hayn, 1724-82; tr. composite
Tune: **Weil ich Jesu Schäflein bin**, Brüder Choral-Buch, 1784

I Am Trusting You, Lord Jesus 126

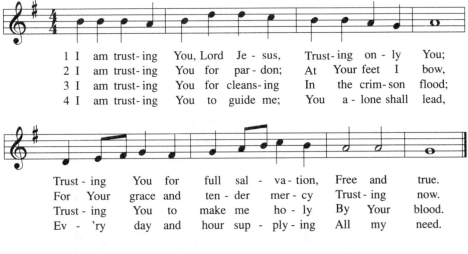

1 I am trust-ing You, Lord Je - sus, Trust-ing on - ly You;
2 I am trust-ing You for par - don; At Your feet I bow,
3 I am trust-ing You for cleans-ing In the crim-son flood;
4 I am trust-ing You to guide me; You a - lone shall lead,

Trust - ing You for full sal - va - tion, Free and true.
For Your grace and ten - der mer - cy Trust - ing now.
Trust - ing You to make me ho - ly By Your blood.
Ev - 'ry day and hour sup - ply - ing All my need.

5 I am trusting You for power;
You can never fail.
Words which You Yourself shall give me
Must prevail.

6 I am trusting You, Lord Jesus;
Never let me fall.
I am trusting You forever
And for all.

Text: Francis R. Havergal, 1836-79, alt.
Tune: **Stephanos**, *Henry W. Baker, 1821-77*

I Know that My Redeemer Lives 127

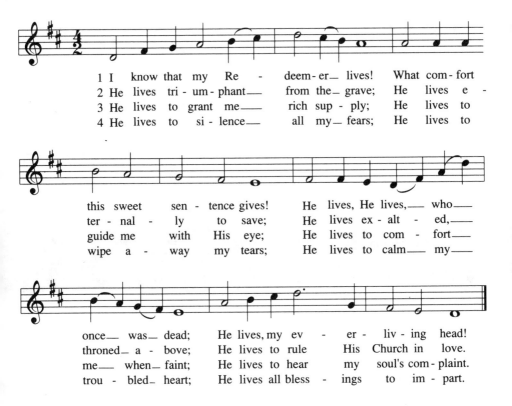

1 I know that my Re - deem-er— lives! What com-fort
2 He lives tri - um - phant— from the— grave; He lives e -
3 He lives to grant me— rich sup - ply; He lives to
4 He lives to si - lence— all my— fears; He lives to

this sweet sen - tence gives! He lives, He lives,— who—
ter - nal - ly to save; He lives ex - alt - ed,—
guide me with His eye; He lives to com - fort—
wipe a - way my tears; He lives to calm— my—

once— was— dead; He lives, my ev - er - liv - ing head!
throned— a - bove; He lives to rule His Church in love.
me— when— faint; He lives to hear my soul's com - plaint.
trou - bled— heart; He lives all bless - ings to im - part.

5 He lives to bless me with His love;
He lives to plead for me above;
He lives my hungry soul to feed;
He lives to help in time of need.

6 He lives, my kind, wise, heav'nly friend;
He lives and loves me to the end;
He lives, and while He lives, I'll sing;
He lives, my Prophet, Priest, and King!

7 He lives and grants me daily breath;
He lives, and I shall conquer death;
He lives my mansion to prepare;
He lives to bring me safely there.

8 He lives, all glory to His name!
He lives, my Savior, still the same;
What joy this blest assurance gives:
I know that my Redeemer lives!

Text: Samuel Medley, 1738-99, alt.
*Tune: **Duke Street**, attr. John Hatton, d. 1793*

128   I Love to Tell the Story

1 I love to tell the sto - ry Of
2 I love to tell the sto - ry, 'Tis
3 I love to tell the sto - ry, For
4 I love to tell the sto - ry, Of

un - seen things a - bove, Of Je - sus and His
pleas - ant to re - peat What seems, each time I
those who know it best Seem hun - ger - ing and
how, from heav'n a - bove Our Lord and Sav - ior

glo - ry, Of Je - sus and His love. I
tell it, More won - der - ful - ly sweet. I
thirst - ing To hear it like the rest. And
Je - sus Was sent to show God's love To

love to tell the sto - ry, Be - cause I know it's true; It
love to tell the sto - ry, For some have nev - er heard The
when in scenes of glo - ry I sing the new, new, song, 'Twill
ev - 'ry sin - ful crea - ture Up - on this earth - ly place How

sat - is - fies my long-ings As noth - ing else would do.
mes - sage of sal - va - tion From God's own ho - ly Word.
be the old, old sto - ry That I have loved so long.
Christ, the gift from heav - en, Is God's great gift of grace.

Refrain

I love to tell the sto-ry; 'Twill be my theme in glo-ry To tell the old, old sto-ry Of Je-sus and His love.

5 I love to tell the story Of our dear Savior's birth.
Of how the angel chorus Announced with joyful mirth
That little baby, Jesus, Was Christ the earth's true Lord.
Of how the lowly shepherds On bended knees adored. *Refrain*

6 I love to tell the story Of how He was baptized.
How God's great voice from heaven Spoke loudly from the skies.
How God the Holy Spirit Descended as a dove.
How Jesus heard His Father Proclaim to all His love. *Refrain*

7 I love to tell the story Of how the people came
To see Him feed the hungry To see Him cure the lame.
For Jesus shows compassion To those in storm and strife
And offers all His children His gift—eternal life. *Refrain*

8 I love to tell the story Although it's sad to tell.
Of how our Lord and Master Faced pain and death and hell.
Dear Jesus, whipped and bleeding Was hung upon the tree
And died on that Good Friday To save both you and me. *Refrain*

9 I love to tell the story Of how our Lord and friend.
Rose up on Easter morning And reigns in highest heav'n.
The love of God the Father, The Spirit, and the Son
Has given us salvation The free gift Jesus won. *Refrain*

©*Text: Arabella Katherine Hankey, 1834-1911, st. 1-3; Jeffrey E. Burkart, st. 4-9*
Tune: **Hankey,** *William Gustavus Fischer, 1835-1912*

129

I Love You, Lord

I love You, Lord, and I lift my voice To wor-ship You, O my soul re-joice. Take joy, my King, in___ what You hear, May it be a sweet, sweet___ sound in___ Your ear.

I Shall Not Be Moved

130

I shall not be, I shall not be moved.

I shall not be, I shall not be moved; Like a

tree plant-ed by the wa-ter, I shall not be moved.

1 When my cross is heav-y, I shall not be moved,
2 The church of God is march-ing, I shall not be moved, The
3 King Je-sus is our Cap-tain, I shall not be moved, King
4 Come on and join the ar-my, I shall not be moved, Come

D. S.

When my cross is heav-y, I shall not be moved; Like a
church of God is march-ing, I shall not be moved; Like a
Je-sus is the Cap-tain, I shall not be moved; Like a
on and join the ar-my, I shall not be moved; Like a

5 Fighting sin and Satan, I shall not be moved,
Fighting sin and Satan, I shall not be moved; Like a

6 When my burden's heavy, I shall not be moved,
When my burden's heavy, I shall not be moved; Like a

7 Don't let the world deceive you, I shall not be moved,
Don't let the world deceive you, I shall not be moved; Like a

8 If my friends forsake me, I shall not be moved,
If my friends forsake me, I shall not be moved; Like a

Text: Afro-American spiritual
Tune: Afro-American spiritual

131   I Sing a Song of the Saints of God

1 I sing a song of the saints of God
2 They loved their Lord so dear, so dear, And
3 They lived not on - ly in a - ges past, There are

Pa - tient and brave and true, Who toiled and fought and
his love made them strong; And they fol - lowed the right for
hun - dreds of thou - sands still, The world is bright with the

lived and died For the Lord they loved and knew. And
Je - sus' sake, The whole of their good lives long. And
joy - ous saints Who love to do Je - sus' will. You can

one was a doc - tor, and one was a queen, and
one was a sol - dier, and one was a priest, and
meet them in school or in lanes, or at sea, In

one was a shep - herd - ess on the green; They were
one was slain by a fierce wild beast: And there's
church, or in trains, or in shops, or at tea, For the

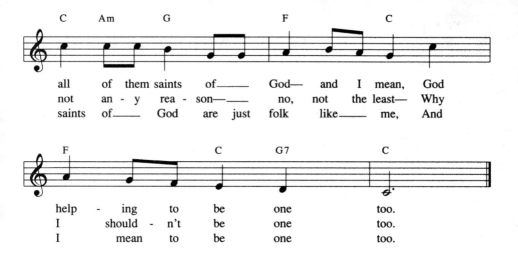

	C	Am	G			F			C
all	of	them	saints	of____		God—	and	I	mean, God
not	an - y	rea -	son—____			no,	not	the least—	Why
saints	of____	God	are	just		folk	like____	me,	And

	F			C	G7		C
help	- ing	to	be	one		too.
I	should -	n't	be	one		too.
I	mean	to	be	one		too.

©Text: Lesbia Scott, b. 1898
©Tune: **Grand Isle**, John Henry Hopkins, 1861-1945

132 I Was Made a Christian

1 I was made a Chris - tian When my name was giv'n,
2 I must, like a Chris - tian, Shun all e - vil ways,
3 All a Chris-tian's bless - ings I will claim for mine:

One of God's dear chil - dren And an heir of heav'n.
Keep my faith in Je - sus, Serve Him all my days.
Ho - ly work and wor - ship, Fel - low - ship di - vine.

In the name of Chris - tian I will glo - ry now,
Called to be a Chris - tian, I will praise the Lord,
Fa - ther, Son, and Spir - it, Give me grace that I

Ev - er - more re - mem - ber My bap - tis - mal vow.
Seek for His as - sis - tance, So to keep my word.
Now may live a Chris - tian And a Chris - tian die.

Text: John Samuel Jones, 1831-1911
*Tune: **Adoro te devote**, mode V, Processionale, Paris, 1697*

I Will Sing of the Mercies

133

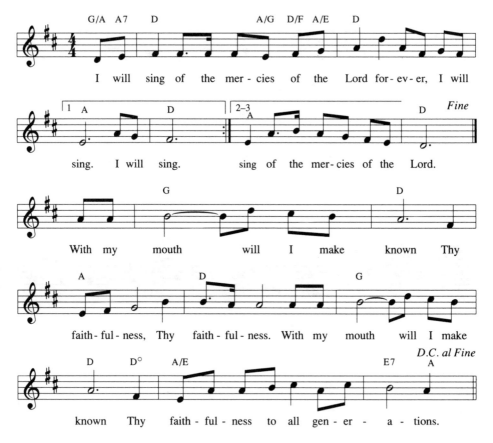

I will sing of the mer-cies of the Lord for-ev-er, I will

1 sing. I will sing. **2–3** sing of the mer-cies of the Lord. *Fine*

With my mouth will I make known Thy

faith-ful-ness, Thy faith-ful-ness. With my mouth will I make

D.C. al Fine

known Thy faith-ful-ness to all gen-er-a-tions.

Text: adapt. from Psalm 89:1
Tune: unknown

134   I'm So Glad, Jesus Lifted Me

1 I'm____ so____ glad,____   Je - sus lift-ed me,
2 Sa - tan had me bound,____
3 When I was in trou - ble,

I'm____ so____ glad,____   Je - sus lift- ed me,
Sa - tan had me bound,____
When I was in trou - ble,

I'm____ so____ glad,____   Je - sus lift-ed me, Sing - ing
Sa - tan had me bound,____
When I was in trou - ble,

Glo - ry, Hal - le - lu - jah!   Je - sus lift - ed me.

Text: Afro-American spiritual
Tune: Afro-American spiritual

In Christ There Is No East or West

1. In Christ there is no east or west, In Him no south or north, But one great fellowship of love Throughout the whole wide earth.

2. In Him shall true hearts ev-'ry-where Their high communion find; His service is the golden cord Close-binding all mankind.

3. Join hands then, brothers of the faith, What-e'er your race may be. Who serves my Father as a son Is surely kin to me.

4. In Christ now meet both east and west, In Him meet south and north; All Christ-ly souls are one in Him Throughout the whole wide earth.

Text: John Oxenham, 1852-1941
©Tune: McKee, Afro-American spiritual; adapt. Harry T. Burleigh, 1866-1949

136 In God We Believe

1 In God we be - lieve: the Cre - a - tor whose pow'r In
2 In Je - sus, the Sav - ior, our hope is se - cured. True
3 God's Spir - it at work in our lives we con - fess; With

mer - cy has brought us for wor - ship this hour. He
God and true man once the cross He en - dured To
pow - er and truth the church now He does bless. As

gra - cious - ly grants us our years and our days And
grant our lives whole - ness, for - give - ness of sin. With
saints, God's for - giv - en, one day we shall then Be

bless - es with kind - ness our work and our ways.
hearts freed from guilt, we know true peace with - in.
liv - ing in glo - ry for - ev - er. A - men.

©Text: Gregory J. Wismar
Tune: **St. Denio**, Welsh folk tune

In You Is Gladness

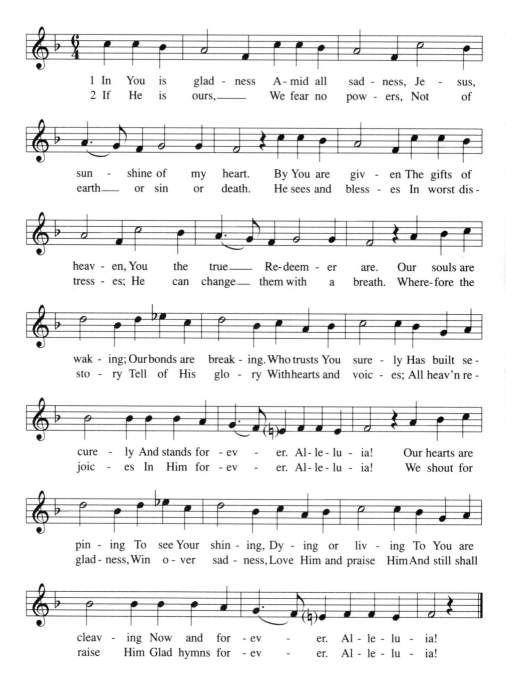

1 In You is glad - ness A - mid all sad - ness, Je - sus,
2 If He is ours,— We fear no pow - ers, Not of

sun - shine of my heart. By You are giv - en The gifts of
earth— or sin or death. He sees and bless - es In worst dis -

heav - en, You the true— Re-deem - er are. Our souls are
tress - es; He can change— them with a breath. Where-fore the

wak - ing; Our bonds are break - ing. Who trusts You sure - ly Has built se -
sto - ry Tell of His glo - ry With hearts and voic - es; All heav'n re -

cure - ly And stands for - ev - er. Al - le - lu - ia! Our hearts are
joic - es In Him for - ev - er. Al - le - lu - ia! We shout for

pin - ing To see Your shin - ing, Dy - ing or liv - ing To You are
glad - ness, Win o - ver sad - ness, Love Him and praise Him And still shall

cleav - ing Now and for - ev - er. Al - le - lu - ia!
raise Him Glad hymns for - ev - er. Al - le - lu - ia!

Text: Johann Lindemann, 1549-1631; tr. Catherine Winkworth, 1829-78, alt.
*Tune: **In dir ist Freude**, Giovanni Giacomo Gastoldi, c. 1556-1622*

138

Infant Holy, Infant Lowly

1 In - fant ho - ly, in - fant low - ly, For His bed a cat - tle stall;
2 Flocks were sleep-ing, shep-herds keep-ing Vig - il till the morn-ing new

Ox - en low - ing, lit - tle know-ing Christ the child is Lord of all.
Saw the glo - ry, heard the sto - ry, Tid - ings of a Gos-pel true.

Swift-ly wing-ing, an - gels sing-ing, Bells are ring-ing, tid-ings bring-ing:
Thus re - joic-ing, free from sor-row, Prais-es voic-ing, greet the mor-row:

Christ the child is Lord of all! Christ the child is Lord of all!
Christ the child was born for you! Christ the child was born for you!

©Text: Polish carol; tr. Edith M. G. Reed, 1885-1933, alt.
Tune: **W zlobie lezy**, Polish carol

I've Got Peace like a River

139

1 I've got peace like a river, I've got
2 I've got joy like a fountain, I've got
3 I've got love like an o - cean, I've got

peace like a riv - er, I've got peace like a
joy like a foun - tain, I've got joy like a
love like an o - cean, I've got love like an

1

riv - er in my soul. I've got
foun - tain in my soul. I've got
o - cean in my soul. I've got

2

riv - er in my soul.
foun - tain in my soul.
o - cean in my soul.

Text: Afro-American spiritual
Tune: Afro-American spiritual

140

1 I've got the joy,— joy,— joy,— joy— down in my heart,
2 I've got the love of Je-sus, love of Je-sus down in my heart,
3 I've got the peace that pass-es un-der-stand-ing down in my heart,
4 I've got the joy,— joy,— joy,— joy— down in my heart,

Down in my heart, down in my heart! I've got the
Down in my heart, down in my heart! I've got the
Down in my heart, down in my heart! I've got the
Down in my heart, down in my heart! I've got the

joy,— joy,— joy,— joy— down in my heart, Down in my heart to stay!
love of Je-sus, love of Je-sus down in my heart, Down in my heart to stay!
peace that pass-es un-der-stand-ing down in my heart, Down in my heart to stay!
joy,— joy,— joy,— joy— down in my heart, Down in my heart to stay!

And it's the great-est, grand-est feel-ing, And it's a

feel-ing here to stay! And it's a joy love that needs re-
peace

veal-ing, So I just want to say:

Text: traditional
*Tune: **Joy Down in My Heart**, traditional*

Jesu, Jesu, Fill Us with Your Love

141

Refrain

Je - su, Je - su, fill us with Your love; Show

us how to serve the neigh - bors We have from You.

1 Kneels at the feet of His friends, Si - lent-ly wash - es their
2 Neigh-bors are rich folk and poor; Neighbors are black, brown, and
3 These are the ones we would serve; These are the ones we would
4 Lov - ing puts us on our knees, Serv - ing as though we were

Refrain

feet, Mas - ter who acts as a slave to them.
white; Neigh - bors are near - by and far a - way.
love; All these are neigh - bors to us and You.
slaves; That is the way we would live with You.

©*Text: Ghanaian; tr. Tom Colvin, b. 1925*
©*Tune: **Chereponi**, Ghana folk song; adapt. Tom Colvin, b. 1925*

142   Jesus Christ Is Risen Today

1 Je - sus Christ is ris'n to-day,
2 Hymns of praise then let us sing,
3 But the pains which He en-dured,
4 Sing we to our God a-bove,

Al - le - lu - ia!

Our tri - um - phant ho - ly day,
Un - to Christ, our heav'n-ly king,
Our sal - va - tion have pro-cured;
Praise e - ter - nal as His love;

Al - le - lu - ia!

Who did once up - on the cross,
Who en - dured the cross and grave,
Now a - bove the sky He's king,
Praise Him, all you heav'n-ly host,

Al - le - lu - ia!

Suf - fer to re - deem our loss.
Sin - ners to re - deem and save.
Where the an - gels ev - er sing.
Fa - ther, Son, and Ho - ly Ghost.

Al - le - lu - ia!

Text: Latin carol, 14th cent., sts. 1-3; Charles Wesley, 1707-88, st. 4; tr. Lyra Davidica, London,
1708, sts. 1-3.
*Tune: **Easter Hymn**, Lyra Davidica, London, 1708*

Jesus in the Morning

143

G

1 Je - sus, Je - sus,
2 Love___ Him, Love___ Him,
3 Serve___ Him, Serve___ Him,
4 Thank___ Him, Thank___ Him,
5 Praise___ Him, Praise___ Him,

C   G

Je - sus in the morn-ing, Je - sus at the noon-time, Je - sus,
Love Him in the morn-ing, Love Him at the noon-time, Love__ Him,
Serve Him in the morn-ing, Serve Him at the noon-time, Serve__ Him,
Thank Him in the morn-ing, Thank Him in the noon-time, Thank__ Him,
Praise Him in the morn-ing, Praise Him in the noon-time, Praise__ Him,

B7   Em   Am7   D   G

Je - sus, Je - sus when the sun goes down.
Love___ Him, Love Him when the sun goes down.
Serve___ Him, Serve Him when the sun goes down.
Thank___ Him, Thank Him when the sun goes down.
Praise___ Him, Praise Him when the sun goes down.

Text: traditional
*Tune: **Jesus in the Morning***

144 Jesus Loves Me, This I Know

1 Je - sus loves me, this I know, For the Bi - ble tells me so.
2 Je - sus loves me, He who died, Heav-en's gate to o - pen wide;

Lit - tle ones to Him be - long; They are weak, but He is strong.
He will wash a - way my sin, Let His lit - tle child come in.

Refrain

Yes, Je - sus loves me, Yes, Je - sus loves me.
Si, Cris - to me a - ma; Si, Cris - to me a - ma;

Yes, Je - sus loves me, The Bi - ble tells me so.
Si, Cris - to me a - ma; La Bi - blia di - ce a - si.

Text: Anna B. Warner, 1820-1915
Tune: William B. Bradbury, 1816-68

Jesus, Name Above All Names 145

1 Je - sus, name a-bove all names, beau-ti-ful
2 Je - sus, lov - ing shep-herd vine of the
3 Je - sus, Way of sal - va - tion, King— of

Sav - ior, glo-ri-ous Lord,_____ Em -
branch - es, Son— of God_____
kings,_____ Lord— of lords,_____ the

man - u - el, God— is with us bless-ed Re -
Prince of Peace, Won-der-ful coun - selor Lord of the
way the truth, and— the Life,_____ Might-y cre -

deem - er,_____ liv - ing Word.
u – ni – verse,_____ Light of the world.
a - tor, My Sav – ior and friend.

146

Jesus, Remember Me

Je-sus, re-mem-ber me when You come in-to Your king - dom. Je - sus, re - mem - ber me when You come in - to Your king - dom.

Text: Luke 23:42
©Tune: Jacques Berthier, b. 1923

Joyful, Joyful We Adore Thee 147

1 Joy - ful, joy - ful we a - dore Thee, God of glo - ry,
2 All Thy works with joy sur - round Thee, Earth and heav'n re -
3 Thou art giv - ing and for - giv - ing, Ev - er bless - ing,

Lord of love! Hearts un - fold like flow'rs be - fore Thee,
flect Thy rays, Stars and an - gels sing a - round Thee,
ev - er blest, Well - spring of the joy of liv - ing,

Prais - ing Thee, their sun a - bove. Melt the clouds of
Cen - ter of un - bro - ken praise. Field and for - est,
O - cean - depth of hap - py rest! Thou our Fa - ther,

sin and sad - ness, Drive the gloom of doubt a - way.
vale and moun - tain, Flow - 'ry mead - ow, flash - ing sea,
Christ our broth - er, All who live in love are Thine;

Giv - er of im - mor - tal glad - ness, Fill us with the light of day.
Chant - ing bird, and flow - ing foun - tain Call us to re - joice in Thee.
Teach us how to love each oth - er, Lift us to the joy di - vine!

Text: Henry van Dyke, 1852-1933
*Tune: **Hymn to Joy**, Ludwig van Beethoven, 1770-1827, adapt.*

Just as I Am

148

1 Just as I am,— with-out— one
2 Just as I am,— though tossed— a-
3 Just as I am,— Thou wilt— re-
4 Just as I am;— Thy love— un-

plea But that— Thy blood was shed for
bout With man - y a con - flict, man - y a
ceive, Wilt wel - come, par - don, cleanse, re-
known Has bro - ken ev - 'ry bar - rier

me And that Thou bidd'st— me come to
doubt, Fight - ings and fears— with - in, with-
lieve; Be - cause Thy prom - ise I be-
down; Now to be Thine,— yea, Thine a-

Thee,—
out,— O Lamb of God,— I come, I come.
lieve,—
lone,—

Text: Charlotte Elliott, 1789-1871
*Tune: **Woodworth**, William B. Bradbury, 1816-68*

149 Keep in Mind that Jesus Christ Has Died for Us

Refrain

C Keep in mind that Je-sus Christ has died for us and is ris-en from the

dead. He is our sav-ing Lord; He is joy for all a - ges.

1 If we die with the Lord, we shall live with the Lord.

Refrain

If we en - dure with the Lord, we shall live with the Lord.

2 In Him all our sor - row, in Him all our joy. In

Refrain

Him hope of glo - ry, in Him all our love.

3 In Him our re - demp - tion, in Him all our grace. In

Him our sal - va - tion, in Him all our peace.

Refrain

Text: from 2 Timothy 2
©*Tune: Lucien Deiss, b. 1921*

150
Kids of the Kingdom

1 Kids of the king - dom, that's what we are:
2 My name is——— I love the Lord.
3 Kids of the king - dom, that's what we are:
4 Praise to the Fa - ther, praise to the Son,

kids of the king - dom, that's what we are.
My name is——— I love the Lord.
kids of the king - dom, that's what we are.
praise to the Spir - it, the Three in One.

We love Je - sus, we love the Lord.
They love Je - sus, they love the Lord.
We love Je - sus, we love the Lord.
We love Je - sus, we love the Lord.

We love Je - sus, we love the Lord.
They love Je - sus, they love the Lord.
We love Je - sus, we love the Lord.
We love Je - sus, we love the Lord.

King of Kings

King of kings and Lord of lords, glo-ry, hal-le-lu-jah!

King of kings and Lord of lords, glo-ry, hal-le-lu-jah!

Je-sus, Prince of Peace, glo-ry, hal-le-lu-jah!

Je-sus, Prince of Peace, glo-ry, hal-le-lu-jah!

152

Knock, Knock

Refrain

Ask, and it shall be giv - en you. Seek, and ye shall find.____ If you

Knock on wood

knock, knock, knock, the door will o - pen un - to you ev' - ry time.

Verses

1 If a son shall ask his fa - ther_ for a piece of bread,
2 If a son shall ask his fa - ther_ for a lit - tle fish,
3 If a son shall ask his fa - ther for an egg____ o - ver light,

will that fa - ther give his__ son__ a stone in - stead?
will that fa - ther give him a ser - pent in his dish?
will that fa - ther give him a scor - pi - on that can bite?

4 If ye then, be-ing e-vil, know how to give good things, How much more your lov-ing heav-en-ly Fa-ther brings! Your lov-ing heav-en-ly Fa-ther brings the best gift of all! He gives the Ho-ly Spir-it un-to them that call on Him.—

Refrain

153 Lamb of God, You Take Away

Lamb of God, You take a-way the sin of the world; have mer-cy on us. Lamb of God, You take a-way the sin of the world; have mer-cy on us. Lamb of God, You take a-way the sin of the world; grant us peace.

Text: International Consultation on English Texts
©*Tune: Richard W. Hillert, b. 1923*

Let All Mortal Flesh Keep Silence

154

1 Let all mor-tal flesh keep— si-lence And with fear and
2 King of kings yet born of— Mar-y, As of old on
3 Rank on rank the host of— heav-en Spreads its van-guard
4 At His feet the six-winged— ser-aph, Cher - u - bim with

trem - bling— stand; Pon - der noth - ing earth - ly -
earth He— stood, Lord of lords in hu - man—
on the— way As the Light of Light, de -
sleep - less— eye, Veil their fac - es to the—

mind - ed, For with bless - ing in His— hand
ves - ture, In the bod - y and the— blood,
scend - ing From the realms of end - less— day,
pres - ence As with cease - less voice they— cry:

Christ our God to earth de - scend - ing
He will give to all the faith - ful
Comes the pow'rs of hell to van - quish
"Al - le - lu - ia, al - le - lu - ia!

Comes our hom - age to de - mand.
His own self for heav'n - ly— food.
As the dark - ness clears a - way.
Al - le - lu - ia, Lord Most— High!"

Text: Liturgy of St. James; tr. Gerard Moultrie, 1829-85, alt.
*Tune: **Picardy**, French folk tune, 17th cent.*

155 Let All Things Now Living

1 Let all things now liv-ing A song of thanks-giving To God the Cre - a-tor tri - um-phant-ly raise, Who fash-ioned and made us, Pro - tect - ed and stayed us, Who still guides us on to the end of our days. His ban - ners are o'er us, His light goes be - fore us, A pil - lar of fire shin-ing forth in the

2 His law He en - forc - es, The stars in their cours-es, The sun in his or - bit, o - be - dient - ly shine. The hills and the moun-tains, The riv - ers and foun - tains, The deeps of the o - cean pro - claim Him di - vine. We too should be voic - ing Our love and re - joic - ing; With glad ad - o - ra - tion a song let us

Week 31   Due 4/26

Judges 6:16   The Lord answered,
"I will be with you, and you will strike
down all the Midianites together."

① An angel
told Mary
not to be afraid

② We are & the
Lord's servant

③ He said Mary
was to have
savior people
have been waitin
for thousands
of years

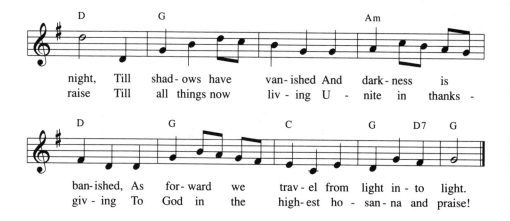

night, Till shad-ows have van-ished And dark-ness is
raise Till all things now liv-ing U - nite in thanks -

ban-ished, As for-ward we trav-el from light in-to light.
giv-ing To God in the high-est ho - san-na and praise!

© Text: Katherine K. Davis, 1892-1980
Tune: **Ashgrove**, Welsh folk tune

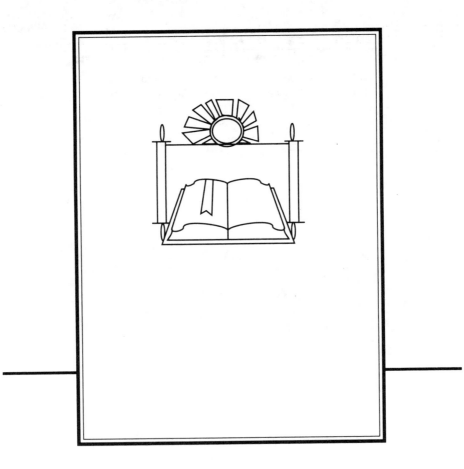

Let Me Learn of Jesus

156

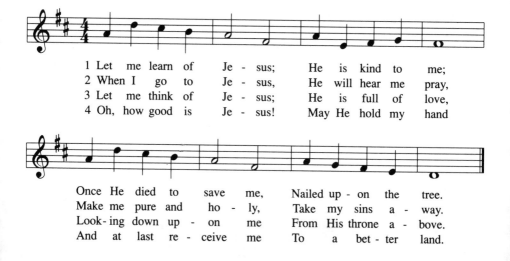

1 Let me learn of Je - sus; He is kind to me;
2 When I go to Je - sus, He will hear me pray,
3 Let me think of Je - sus; He is full of love,
4 Oh, how good is Je - sus! May He hold my hand

Once He died to save me, Nailed up - on the tree.
Make me pure and ho - ly, Take my sins a - way.
Look- ing down up - on me From His throne a - bove.
And at last re - ceive me To a bet - ter land.

Text: Fanny J. Crosby, 1820-1915
*Tune: **Sandown**, James Frederick Swift, 1847-1931*

157 Let My Prayer Rise before You

C Let my prayer rise be-fore You as in-cense;

the lift-ing up of my hands as the eve-ning sac-ri-fice.

I O Lord, I call to You; come to me quick-ly;

hear my voice when I cry to You. II Let my prayer rise be-fore You as in-cense;

the lift-ing up of my hands as the eve-ning sac-ri-fice.

I Set a watch be-fore my mouth, O Lord, and guard the door of my lips.

II Let not my heart in-cline to an-y e-vil thing; Let me

not be oc-cu-pied in wick-ed-ness with e-vil-do-ers.

I But my eyes are turned to You, O God; in You I take ref-uge.

Strip me not of my life. II Glo-ry be to the Fa-ther and to the

Son and to the Ho-ly Spir-it;

I as it was in the be-gin-ning, is now, and will be for-ev-er. A-men.

C Let my prayer rise be-fore You as in-cense;

the lift-ing up of my hands as the eve-ning sac-ri-fice.

158 Let Our Gladness Have No End

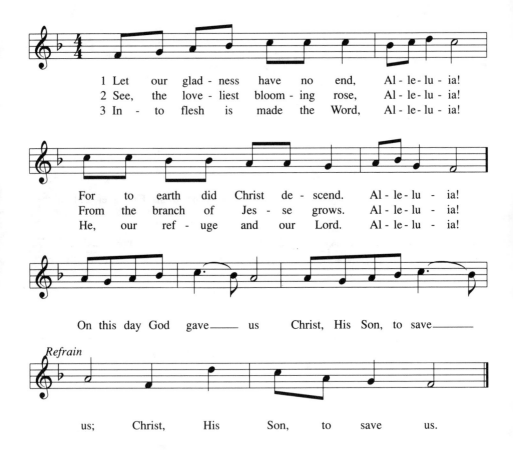

1 Let our glad - ness have no end, Al - le - lu - ia!
2 See, the love - liest bloom - ing rose, Al - le - lu - ia!
3 In - to flesh is made the Word, Al - le - lu - ia!

For to earth did Christ de - scend. Al - le - lu - ia!
From the branch of Jes - se grows. Al - le - lu - ia!
He, our ref - uge and our Lord. Al - le - lu - ia!

On this day God gave us Christ, His Son, to save

Refrain

us; Christ, His Son, to save us.

Text: Bohemian carol, 15th cent.; tr. unknown
Tune: **Narodil se Kristus Pán**, Bohemian carol, 15th cent.

Let Us Ever Walk with Jesus 159

1 Let us ev-er walk with Je-sus, Fol-low His ex - am-ple pure,
2 Let us al-so live with Je-sus. He has ris-en from the dead

Through a world that would de-ceive us And to sin our spir-its lure.
That to life we may a-wak-en. Je - sus, since You are our head,

On-ward in His foot-steps tread-ing, Pil - grims here, our home a-bove,
We are Your own liv - ing mem-bers; Where You live, there we shall be

Full of faith and hope and love, Let us do our Fa-ther's bid-ding.
In Your pres-ence con-stant-ly, Liv-ing there with You for - ev - er.

Faith-ful Lord, with me a-bide; I shall fol-low where You guide.
Je - sus, let me faith-ful be, Life e - ter-nal grant to me.

Text: Sigismund von Birken, 1626-81; tr. Lutheran Book of Worship, *1978, alt.*
Tune: **Lasset uns mit Jesu zeihen**, *Georg G. Boltze, 1788*

160   Life Is a Journey

1 No - ah had nev - er been   sail - ing when God   Said,
2 Wise men were look-ing up   in - to the skies.   They
3 Paul as a pris- 'ner was   shipped off to Rome
4 Laugh-ter or sor-row or   gig - gles or tears;

"Build you an ark   'cause I'm   send - ing a flood   And
saw a new star   which was   quite a sur-prise.   They
Far from his coun - try and   far from his home.   But
Good days or bad   days; great   tri - umphs or fears.   Oh,

take ev - 'ry an - i - mal   on - to the boat."
fol - lowed that star with its   light stream-ing down.
Paul knew the Lord as his   friend and his guide.
what will life's jour - ney be?   We can - not know.

God blessed their jour - ney and   kept them a - float.
God blessed their jour - ney in   Beth - le - hem town.
God blessed his jour - ney and   stayed by his side.
Lord, bless our jour - ney, wher - ev - er we go.

Refrain

F   **C**

Life is a jour - ney we're tak - in' each day.

G   **C**

Life is a jour - ney and we're on our way. And

F   **C**

God in His mer - cy from heav - en a - bove

G7   **C**   *Fine*

Bless - es our jour - ney in love!

161 Lift Every Voice and Sing

1 Lift ev - 'ry voice and sing Till earth and heav - en
2 Ston - y the road we trod, Bit - ter the chas-t'ning
3 God of our wea - ry years, God of our si - lent

ring, Ring with the har - mo - nies of lib - er -
rod, Felt in the days when hope un - born had
tears, Thou who hast brought us thus far on the

ty. Let our re - joic - ing rise High as the lis - t'ning
died; Yet, with a stead - y beat, Have not our wea - ry
way; Thou who hast by Thy might Led us in - to the

skies; Let it re -sound loud as the roll - ing sea.
feet Come to the place for which our par - ents sighed?
light; Keep us for - ev - er in the path, we pray.

Sing a song full of the faith that the dark past has taught us;
We have come o - ver a way that with tears has been wa - tered;
Lest our feet stray from the plac- es, our God, where we met thee;

Sing a song full of the hope that the pres - ent has brought
We have come, tread - ing our path through the blood of the slaugh -
Lest, our hearts drunk with the wine of the world, we for - get

us; Fac - ing the ris - ing sun Of our new day be-
tered, Out from the gloom - y past, Till now we stand at
Thee; Shad-owed be - neath Thy hand May we for - ev - er

gun, Let us march on, till vic - to - ry is won.
last Where the white gleam of our bright star is cast.
stand, True to our God, true to our na - tive land.

©Text: James W. Johnson, 1871-1938
©Tune: **Lift Ev'ry Voice and Sing,** J. Rosamond Johnson, 1873-1954

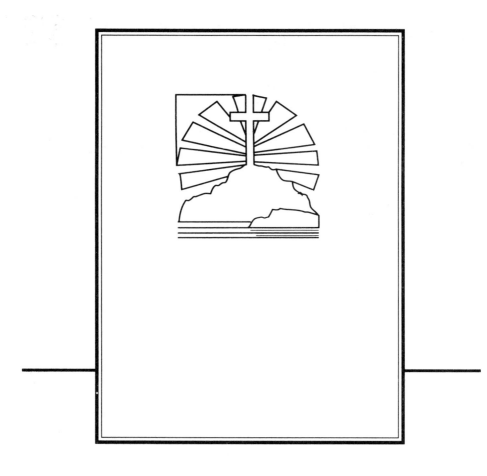

Lift High the Cross

162

Refrain

Lift high the cross, the love of Christ pro - claim Till
all the world _____ a- dore _____ His sa - cred name.

1 Come, Chris-tians, fol - low where our cap - tain trod,
2 Led on their way by this tri - um - phant sign,
3 All new - born sol - diers of the Cru - ci - fied
4 O Lord, once lift - ed on the glo - rious tree,

Our king vic - to - rious, Christ, the Son of God.
The hosts of God in con - qu'ring ranks com - bine.
Bear on their brows the seal of Him who died.
Raise us, and let Your cross the mag - net be.

5 So shall our song of triumph ever be:
  Praise to the Crucified for victory! *Refrain*

©Text: George W. Kitchin, 1827-1912; Michael R. Newbolt, 1874-1956, alt.
©Tune: **Crucifer**, Sydney H. Nicholson, 1875-1947

163   Light One Candle

1 Light one can-dle for hope,   one bright can-dle for
2 Light one can-dle for peace,   one bright can-dle for
3 Light one can-dle for love,   one bright can-dle for

hope,   He brings hope to ev - 'ry heart, He
peace,   He brings peace to ev - 'ry heart, He
love,   He brings love to ev - 'ry heart, He

comes!   He comes!   comes!   He

comes!   Light one can-dle for joy,

one bright can-dle for joy,   Ev - 'ry na-tion will

find sal - va-tion in Beth-l'em's ba - by boy.

comes! He comes! He brings love to

ev - 'ry heart, He comes! He comes!

164 Listen! You Nations

Refrain

Lis-ten! you na-tions of the world: lis-ten to the Word of the Lord. An-
nounce it from coast to coast; de - clare it to dis - tant is - lands.

1 The Lord who scat-tered Is-ra-el will gath-er His peo-ple a-gain; and
He will keep watch o-ver them as a shep-herd watch-es his flock. *Refrain*

2 With shouts of joy they will come, their fac-es ra-diant-ly hap-py, for the
Lord is so gen-'rous to them; He show-ers His peo-ple with gifts. *Refrain*

3 Young wom-en will dance for joy, and men young and old will make mer-ry like a

gar - den re-freshed by the rain, they will nev-er be in want a-gain.

Break in-to shouts of great joy: Ja-cob is free a - gain! Teach

na-tions to sing the song: "The Lord has saved His peo-ple!"

165

Lord, Be Glorified

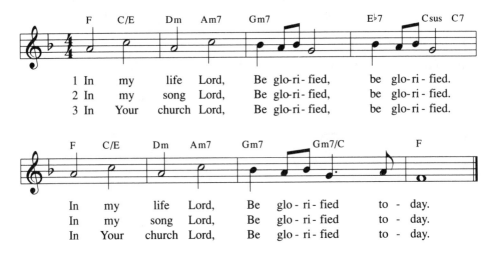

1 In my life Lord, Be glo-ri-fied, be glo-ri-fied.
2 In my song Lord, Be glo-ri-fied, be glo-ri-fied.
3 In Your church Lord, Be glo-ri-fied, be glo-ri-fied.

In my life Lord, Be glo - ri - fied to - day.
In my song Lord, Be glo - ri - fied to - day.
In Your church Lord, Be glo - ri - fied to - day.

Lord, I Want to Be a Christian 166

1 Lord, I want to be a Chris-tian In my heart, in my
2 Lord, I want to be more lov - ing In my heart, in my
3 Lord, I want to be more ho - ly In my heart, in my
4 Lord, I want to be like Je - sus In my heart, in my

heart;— Lord, I want to be a Chris-tian In my heart,
heart;— Lord, I want to be more lov - ing In my heart,
heart;— Lord, I want to be more ho - ly In my heart,
heart;— Lord, I want to be like Je - sus In my heart,

In my heart,————— In my heart,—————
In my heart, In my

Lord, I want to be a Chris-tian In my heart.
Lord, I want to be more lov - ing In my heart.
heart, Lord, I want to be more ho - ly In my heart.
Lord, I want to be like Je - sus In my heart.

Text: Afro-American spiritual
Tune: Afro-American spiritual

167   Lord of All Hopefulness

1 Lord of all hope-ful-ness, Lord of all joy, Whose
2 Lord of all ea-ger-ness, Lord of all faith, Whose
3 Lord of all kind-li-ness, Lord of all grace, Your
4 Lord of all gen-tle-ness, Lord of all calm, Whose

trust, ev-er child-like, no cares could de-stroy: Be
strong hands were skilled at the plane and the lathe: Be
hands swift to wel-come, your arms to em-brace: Be
voice is con-tent-ment, whose pres-ence is balm: Be

there at our wak-ing, and give us, we pray, Your
there at our la-bors, and give us, we pray, Your
there at our hom-ing, and give us, we pray, Your
there at our sleep-ing, and give us, we pray, Your

bliss in our hearts, Lord, at the break of the day.
strength in our hearts, Lord, at the noon of the day.
love in our hearts, Lord, at the eve of the day.
peace in our hearts, Lord, at the end of the day.

© Text: Jan Struther, 1901-53
Tune: **Slane**, Irish folk tune

Lord of All Nations, Grant Me Grace

168

1 Lord of all na - tions, grant me grace To
2 Break down the wall that would di - vide Thy
3 For - give me, Lord, where I have erred By
4 Give me Thy cour - age, Lord, to speak When -

love all peo - ple, ev - 'ry race And in each mor - tal
chil - dren, Lord, on ev - 'ry side. My neigh-bor's good let
love - less act and thought-less word. Make me to see the
ev - er strong op - press the weak. Should I my - self the

may I see My kin - dred, loved, re - deemed by Thee.
me pur - sue, Let Chris - tian love bind warm and true.
wrong I do Will cru - ci - fy my Lord a - new.
vic - tim be, Help me for - give, re - mem - b'ring Thee.

5 With Thine own love may I be filled
And by Thy Holy Spirit willed,
That all I touch, whate'er I be,
May be divinely touched by Thee.

©Text: Olive Wise Spannaus, b. 1916, alt.
Tune: **Tallis' Canon**, Thomas Tallis, c. 1505-85

169

Lord of Glory, You Have Bought Us

1 Lord of glo - ry, You have bought us
2 Grant us hearts, dear Lord, to give You
3 Lord of glo - ry, You have bought us

With Your life - blood as the price,
Glad - ly, free - ly of Your own.
With Your life - blood as the price,

Nev - er grudg - ing for the lost ones
With the sun - shine of Your good - ness
Nev - er grudg - ing for the lost ones

That tre - men - dous sac - ri - fice;
Melt our thank - less hearts of stone
That tre - men - dous sac - ri - fice.

And with that have free - ly giv - en
Till our cold and self - ish na - tures,
Give us faith to trust You bold - ly,

Bless - ings count - less as the sand
Warmed by You, at length be - lieve
Hope, to stay our souls on You;

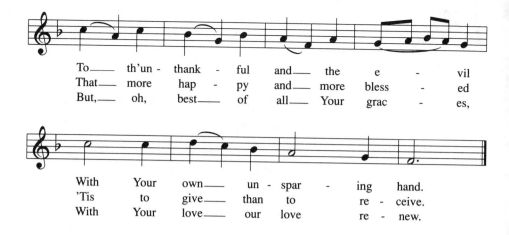

To— th'un - thank - ful and— the e - vil
That— more hap - py and— more bless - ed
But,— oh, best— of all— Your grac - es,

With Your own— un - spar - ing hand.
'Tis to give— than to re - ceive.
With Your love— our love re - new.

Text: Eliza S. Alderson, 1818-89, alt.
Tune: **Hyfrydol,** Rowland H. Prichard, 1811-87

170   Lord of the Dance

lead you all wher - ev - er you may be, and I'll

lead you all in the dance, said He.

5 They cut me down and I leapt up high,
I am the life that'll never, never die;
I'll live in you if you'll live in Me;
I am the Lord of the Dance, said He.

© Text: *Sydney Carter, 1963*
Tune: **Lord of the Dance,** *Shaker tune, 19th cent.; adapt. by Sydney Carter, b. 1915*

171 Lord, Take My Hand and Lead Me

1 Lord, take my hand and lead me Up - on life's way;
2 Lord, when the tem - pest ra - ges, I need not fear;
3 Lord, when the shad - ows length - en And night has come,

Di - rect, pro - tect, and feed me From day to day.
For You, the Rock of A - ges, Are al - ways near.
I know that You will strength - en My steps toward home,

With - out Your grace and fa - vor I go a - stray;
Close by Your side a - bid - ing, I fear no foe,
And noth - ing can im - pede me, O bless - ed Friend!

So take my hand, O Sav - ior, And lead the way.
For when Your hand is guid - ing, In peace I go.
So, take my hand and lead me Un - to the end.

© Text: Julie von Hausmann, 1925-1901; tr. Lutheran Book of Worship, 1978
Tune: **So nimm denn meine Hände,** Frederich Silcher 1789-1869

Lord, Whose Love in Humble Service

172

F   B♭   Am7   Dm   F

1 Lord, whose love in hum - ble ser - vice Bore the
2 Still Your chil - dren wan - der home - less; Still the
3 As we wor - ship, grant us vi - sion, Till Your

B♭   F   F   B♭   Am7

weight of hu - man need, Who up - on the cross, for -
hun - gry cry for bread; Still the cap - tives long for
love's re - veal - ing light In its height and depth and

Dm   F   B♭   F   F

sak - en, Worked Your mer - cy's per - fect deed: We, Your
free - dom; Still in grief we mourn our dead. As You,
great - ness Dawns up - on our quick - ened sight, Mak - ing

C   Dm   C Dm

ser - vants, bring the wor - ship Not of voice a - lone, but
Lord, in deep com - pas - sion Healed the sick and freed the
known the needs and bur - dens Your com - pas - sion bids us

B♭maj7   C   Dm

heart; Con - se - crat - ing to Your
soul, By Your Spir - it send Your
bear, Stir - ring us to ar - dent

B♭   F   Gm7 Am Gm7   F

pur - pose Ev - 'ry gift which You im - part.
pow - er To our world to make it whole.
ser - vice, Your a - bun - dant life to share.

© Text: Albert F. Bayly, 1901-84, alt.
Tune: **Beach Spring**, The Sacred Harp, *Philadelphia, 1844.*

173

Lord's Prayer

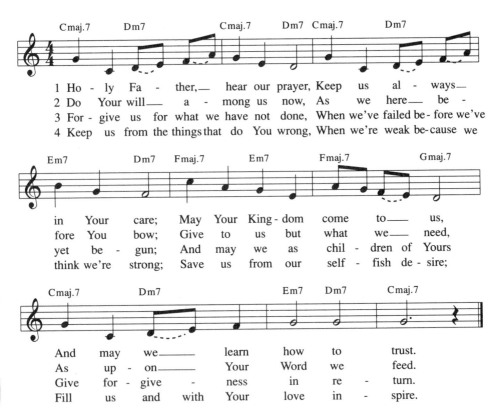

1 Ho - ly Fa - ther,— hear our prayer, Keep us al - ways—
2 Do Your will— a - mong us now, As we here— be -
3 For - give us for what we have not done, When we've failed be- fore we've
4 Keep us from the things that do You wrong, When we're weak be-cause we

in Your care; May Your King - dom come to— us,
fore You bow; Give to us but what we— need,
yet be - gun; And may we as chil - dren of Yours
think we're strong; Save us from our self - fish de - sire;

And may we— learn how to trust.
As up - on— Your Word we feed.
Give for - give - ness in re - turn.
Fill us and with Your love in - spire.

5 Honor, greatness belong to You,
Love and peace and mercy, too!
Praise to You again and again!
Amen.

Make Me a Servant   174

Make me a ser- vant, hum- ble and meek,

Lord, let me lift up those who are weak.

And may the pray'r of my heart al- ways be:

Make me a ser- vant, make me a ser- vant,

make me a ser- vant to- day.

175   My Faith Looks Trustingly

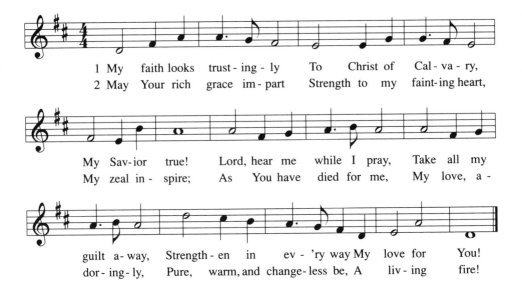

1 My faith looks trust-ing-ly To Christ of Cal-va-ry,
2 May Your rich grace im-part Strength to my faint-ing heart,

My Sav-ior true! Lord, hear me while I pray, Take all my
My zeal in-spire; As You have died for me, My love, a-

guilt a-way, Strength-en in ev-'ry way My love for You!
dor-ing-ly, Pure, warm, and change-less be, A liv-ing fire!

Text: Ray Palmer, 1808-87, alt.
*Tune: **Olivet**, Lowell Mason, 1792-1872*

My Song Is Love Unknown 176

1 My song is love un - known, My Sav - ior's love to
2 He came from His blest throne, Sal - va - tion to be -
3 Some times they strew His way And His sweet prais- es
4 Why, what hath my Lord done? What makes this rage and

me, Love to the love - less shown That they might
stow; But men made strange, and none The longed - for
sing; Re - sound - ing all the day Ho - san - nas
spite? He made the lame to run, He gave the

love - ly be. Oh, who am I That
Christ would know. But oh, my Friend, My
to their King. Then "Cru - ci - fy!" Is
blind their sight. Sweet in - ju - ries! Yet

for my sake The Lord should take Frail flesh and die?
friend in - deed, Who at my need His life did spend!
all their breath, And for His death They thirst and cry.
they at these Them- selves dis - please And 'gainst Him rise.

5 They rise and needs will have
My dear Lord made away;
A murderer they save,
The prince of life they slay.
Yet cheerful He
To suff'ring goes
That He His foes
From thence might free.

6 In life no house, no home
My Lord on earth might have;
In death no friendly tomb
But what a stranger gave.
What may I say?
Heav'n was His home
But mine the tomb
Wherein He lay.

7 Here might I stay and sing,
No story so divine!
Never was love, dear King,
Never was grief like Thine.
This is my friend,
In whose sweet praise
I all my days
Could gladly spend!

Text: Samuel Crossman, c. 1624-83
©Tune: **Love Unknown**, *John Ireland, 1879-1962*

My Soul Now Magnifies the Lord

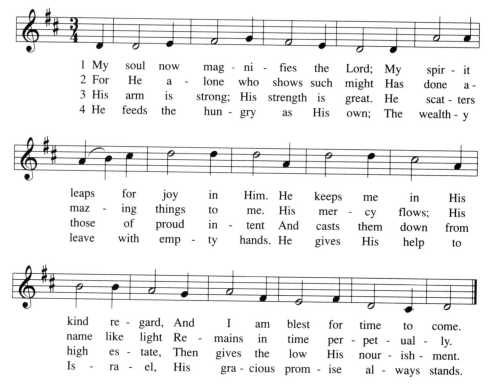

1 My soul now mag - ni - fies the Lord; My spir - it
2 For He a - lone who shows such might Has done a -
3 His arm is strong; His strength is great. He scat - ters
4 He feeds the hun - gry as His own; The wealth - y

leaps for joy in Him. He keeps me in His
maz - ing things to me. His mer - cy flows; His
those of proud in - tent And casts them down from
leave with emp - ty hands. He gives His help to

kind re - gard, And I am blest for time to come.
name like light Re - mains in time per - pet - ual - ly.
high es - tate, Then gives the low His nour - ish - ment.
Is - ra - el, His gra - cious prom - ise al - ways stands.

© Text: Luke 1:46-55; versification, Stephanie K. Frey, b. 1952
Tune: **Puer nobis,** adapt. Michael Praetorius, 1571-1621

178 My Soul Proclaims the Greatness

My soul pro-claims the great-ness of the Lord;

my spir-it re-joic-es in God my Sav-ior,

for He has looked with fa-vor on His low-ly ser-vant.

From this day all gen-er-a-tions will call me bless-ed.

The Al-might-y has done great things for me, and ho-ly is His name.

He has mer-cy on those who fear Him in ev-'ry gen-er-a-tion.

He has shown the strength of His arm; He has scat-tered the proud in their con ceit.

He has cast down the might-y from their thrones and has lift-ed up the low-ly.

He has filled the hun-gry with good things, and the rich He has sent a-way emp-ty.

He has come to the help of His ser-vant Is-ra-el,

for He has re-mem-bered His prom-ise of mer-cy,

the prom-ise He made to our fa-thers,

to A-bra-ham and His chil-dren for-ev-er.

Glo-ry be to the Fa-ther and to the Son and to the Ho-ly Spir-it;

as it was in the be-gin-ning, is now, and will be for-ev-er. A-men.

Text: International Consultation on English Texts
©*Tune: Dale Wood. b. 1934*

179   My Tribute

To God be the glo - ry, to God be the glo - ry, to God be the glo - ry for the things He has done. With His blood He has saved me; with His pow'r He has raised me; to God be the glo - ry for the things He has done.

New Testament Song

180

Mat-thew, Mark and Luke and John, Acts, Ro-mans, First and Sec-ond Cor-in-thi-ans, Ga - la-tians, E-phe-sians, Phil - ip - pi-ans, Col-os-sians, First and Sec-ond Thes-sa - lo - ni-ans, First Tim - o-thy, Sec-ond Tim - o-thy, Ti-tus, Phi - le-mon, He-brews, James,—— First Pe-ter, Sec-ond Pe-ter, three Johns, Jude and Re-vel - a - tion.

Text: unknown
Tune: unknown

181 Now Thank We All Our God

1 Now thank we all our God With hearts and hands and voic-es,
2 Oh, may this boun-teous God Through all our life be near us,
3 All praise and thanks to God The Fa-ther now be giv-en,

Who won-drous things has done, In whom His world re - joic-es;
With ev - er joy - ful hearts And bless-ed peace to cheer us
The Son, and Him who reigns With them in high-est heav-en,

Who from our moth-er's arms Has blest us on our way With
And keep us in His grace And guide us when per-plexed And
The one e - ter - nal God, Whom earth and heav'n a - dore; For

count - less gifts of love And still is ours to - day.
free us from all harm In this world and the next!
thus it was, is now, And shall be ev - er - more.

Text: Martin Rinckart, 1586-1649; tr. Catherine Winkworth, 1829-78
Tune: **Nun danket alle Gott**, Johann Crüger, 1598-1662

O God of Mercy, God of Light   182

1 O God of mer - cy, God of light,
In love and mer - cy in - fi - nite,
Teach us, as ev - er in Your sight,
To live our lives in You.

2 You sent Your Son to die for all
That our lost world might hear Your call;
Oh, hear us lest we stray and fall!
We rest our hope in You.

3 Teach us the les - son Je - sus taught:
To feel for those His blood has bought,
That ev - 'ry deed and word and thought
May work a work for You.

4 For all are kin - dred, far and wide,
Since Je - sus Christ for all has died;
Grant us the will and grace pro - vide
To love them all in You.

5 In sickness, sorrow, want, or care,
Each other's burdens help us share;
May we, where help is needed, there
Give help as though to You.

6 And may Your Holy Spirit move
All those who live to live in love
Till You receive in heav'n above
Those who have lived to You.

Text: Godfrey Thring, 1823-1903
*Tune: **Just as I Am**, Joseph Barnby, 1838-96, adapt.*

183 O Little Town of Bethlehem

1 O lit-tle town of Beth-le-hem, How
2 For Christ is born of Mar - y, And,
3 How si-lent-ly, how si-lent-ly The
4 O ho-ly Child of Beth-le-hem, De-

still we see Thee lie! A - bove Thy deep And
gath-ered all a - bove While mor-tals sleep, The
won-drous gift is giv'n! So God im-parts To
scend to us, we pray; Cast out our sin, And

dream-less sleep The si-lent stars go by; Yet
an - gels keep Their watch of won-d'ring love. O
hu - man hearts The bless-ings of his heav'n. No
en - ter in, Be born in us to - day. We

in Thy dark streets shin - eth The
morn - ing stars, to - geth - er Pro -
ear may hear His com - ing; But
hear the Christ - mas an - gels The

ev - er - last - ing light. The hopes and fears Of
claim the ho - ly birth, And prais - es sing To
in this world of sin, Where meek souls will Re -
great glad ti - dings tell; Oh, come to us, A -

all the years Are met in Thee to - night.
God the king And peace to all the earth!
ceive Him, still The dear Christ en - ters in.
bide with us, Our Lord Im - man - u - el!

Text: Philips Brooks, 1835-93
*©Tune: **Forest Green**, English traditional melody: coll. and arr. Ralph Vaughan Williams,*
1872-1958

O Lord Jesus, Child of Beauty 184

1 O Lord Je - sus, child of
2 O Lord Je - sus, King of
3 Je - sus, we will sing Your

beau - ty, Born to free us
heav - en, Here on earth you'll
prais - es, Voic - es raised to

from our sin, We will
suf - fer pain To re -
You a - bove, And re -

glad - ly sing Your hon - or
deem us from sin's bon - dage
joice in all Your mer - cies

For the peace we have with - in.
And our hap - pi - ness to gain.
Show - ered down on us in love.

1 ¡Oh Jesús, Niñito hermoso,
   Fuente de la salvación!
   Cantaré tu prez con gozo
   Por la paz del conrazón.

2 ¡Oh Jesús, Señor del cielo,
   Aquí vienes a sufrir!
   A librarme del pecado
   Y a dar dicha a mi vivir.

3 ¡Oh Jesús, te canto alegre
   Con los niños alredor!
   Tu bondad exalto siempre
   Demostrada con amor.

©Text: Héctor Hoppe, 1954; tr. Jaroslav Vajda, b. 1919
©Tune: **Regensberg**, Leónido Krey

185   Oh, Come, All Ye Faithful

1 Oh, come all ye faith - ful, Joy - ful and tri - umphant!
2   High - est, most ho - ly, Light of light e - ter - nal,
3   Sing, choirs of an - gels, Sing in ex - ul - ta - tion,
4   Yea, Lord, we greet thee, Born this hap - py morning;

come ye, oh, come— ye to Beth - le - hem;
Born of a vir - gin, a mor - tal He comes;
Sing, all ye cit - i - zens of heav - en a - bove!
Je - sus, to Thee— be— glo - ry giv'n!

Come and be - hold Him Born the king of an - gels:
Son of the Fa - ther Now in flesh ap - pear - ing!
Glo - ry to God— In— the— high - est:
Word of the Fa - ther, Now in flesh ap - pear - ing

Oh, come, let us a - dore Him, Oh, come, let us a - dore Him, Oh,

come, let us a - dore Him,— Christ— the Lord!

Text: attr. John F. Wade, c. 1711-86; tr. composite
*Tune: **Adeste Fideles**, John F. Wade, c. 1711-86*

Oh, Come, Oh, Come, Emmanuel

186

1 Oh, come, oh, come, Em - man - u -
2 Oh, come, O Rod of Jes - se's
el, And ran - som cap - tive Is - ra - el,
stem, From ev - 'ry foe de - liv - er them
That mourns in lone - ly ex - ile here
That trust Your might - y pow'r to save;
Un - til the Son of God ap - pear.
Bring them in vic - t'ry through the grave.
Re - joice! Re - joice! Em - man - u - el Shall
Re - joice! Re - joice! Em - man - u - el Shall
come to thee, O Is - ra - el.
come to thee, O Is - ra - el.

Text: Psalteriolum Cantionum Catholicarum, *Köln, 1710; tr. John. M. Neale, 1818-66, alt.*
Tune: ***Veni, Emmanuel,*** *French processional, 15th cent.*

187 Oh, for a Thousand Tongues to Sing

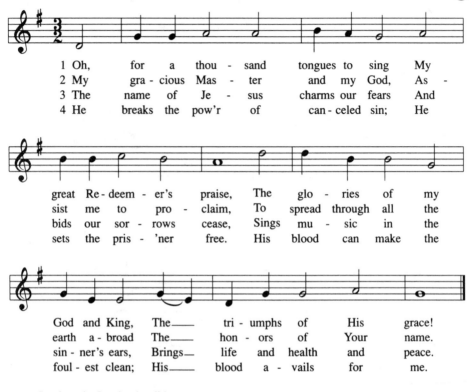

1 Oh, for a thou - sand tongues to sing My
2 My gra - cious Mas - ter and my God, As -
3 The name of Je - sus charms our fears And
4 He breaks the pow'r of can - celed sin; He

great Re - deem - er's praise, The glo - ries of my
sist me to pro - claim, To spread through all the
bids our sor - rows cease, Sings mu - sic in the
sets the pris - 'ner free. His blood can make the

God and King, The—— tri - umphs of His grace!
earth a - broad The—— hon - ors of Your name.
sin - ner's ears, Brings— life and health and peace.
foul - est clean; His—— blood a - vails for me.

5 Look to the Lord, who did atone
For sin, O fallen race,
Look and be saved through faith alone,
Be justified by grace.

6 See all our sins on Jesus laid;
The Lamb has made us whole.
His soul was once an off'ring made
For ev'ry human soul.

7 To God all glory, praise, and love
Be now and ever giv'n
By saints below and saints above,
The Church in earth and heav'n.

Text: Charles Wesley, 1707-88, alt.
Tune: **Azmon,** *Carl G. Glazer, 1784-1829*

Oh, He's King of Kings

188

Oh, He's King of kings, Oh, He's Lord of lords!

Je-sus Christ, the First and Last, No man works like Him.

1 I know that my Re-deem-er lives,
2 Vic-to-ri-ous at God's right hand, No man works like Him,

And by His love sweet blessings gives,
He calls His saints from ev-'ry land, No man works like Him.

Tune: American spiritual
*Text: **King of Kings**, American spiritual*

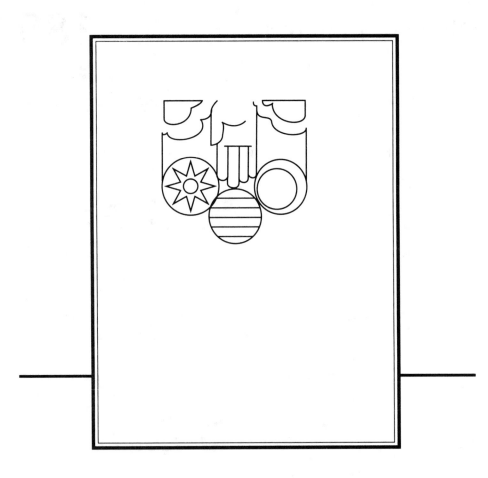

Oh, Sing to the Lord

189

1 Oh, sing to the Lord, Oh, sing God a new song, Oh,
2 For God is the Lord And He has done won ders. For
1 Can- tad al Se - ñor un cán - ti - co nue- vo, Can-
2 Por- que el Se - ñor ha he- cho pro - di- gios, Por -

sing to the Lord, Oh, sing God a new song. Oh,
God is the Lord And He has done won - ders. For
tad al Se - ñor un cán - ti - co nue - vo, Can -
que el Se - ñor ha he - cho pro - di - gios, Por -

sing to the Lord, Oh, sing God a new song. Oh,
God is the Lord And He has done won - ders.
tad al Se - ñor un cán - ti - co nue - vo.
que el Se - ñor ha he - cho pro - di - gios. ¡Can -

sing to our God. Oh, sing to our God.
tad al Se - ñor, can - tad al Se - ñor!

©*Text: Psalm 98; adapt. G. Cartford, b. 1923*
Tune: Brazilian folk song

190   Oh, that I Had a Thousand Voices

1 Oh, that I had a thou-sand voic - es
2 O all you pow'rs that He im - plant - ed,
3 You for - est leaves so green and ten - der
4 All crea-tures that have breath and mo - tion,

To praise my God with thou - sand tongues!
A - rise, keep si - lence now no more;
That dance for joy in sum - mer air,
That throng the earth, the sea, the sky,

My heart, which in the Lord re - joic - es,
Put forth the strength that God has grant - ed!
You mead - ow grass - es, bright and slen - der,
Come, share with me my heart's de - vo - tion,

Would then pro - claim in grate - ful songs
Your no - blest work is to a - dore.
You flow'rs so fra - grant and so fair,
Help me to sing God's prais - es high.

To all, wher - ev - er I might be, What
O soul and bod - y, join to raise With
You live to show God's praise a - lone. Join
My ut - most pow'rs can nev - er quite De -

great	things	God	has		done	for	me.
heart -	felt	joy	our		mak -	er's	praise.
me	to	make	His		glo -	ry	known.
clare	the	won	-	ders	of	His	might.

5 Creator, humbly I implore You
   To listen to my earthly song
   Until that day when I adore You,
   When I have joined the angel throng
   And learned with choirs of heav'n to sing
   Eternal anthems to my King!

Text: Johann Mentzer, 1658-1734; tr. The Lutheran Hymnal, *1941, alt.*
*Tune: **O dass ich tausend Zungen hätte**, Johann B. König, Harmonischer Lieder-Schatz, 1738*

191 Oh, that the Lord Would Guide My Ways

1 Oh, that the Lord would guide my ways To
2 Or - der my foot - steps by Your Word And
3 As - sist my soul, too apt to stray, A
4 Make me to walk in Your com - mands, A

keep His stat - utes still! Oh, that my God would
make my heart sin - cere; Let sin have no do -
strict - er watch to keep; If ev - er I for -
most de - light - ful road; Nor let my head or

grant me grace To know and do His will!
min - ion, Lord, But keep my con - science clear.
get Your way, Re - store Your wan - d'ring sheep.
heart or hands Of - fend a - gainst my God.

Text: Isaac Watts, 1674-1748, alt.
*Tune: **Evan**, William H. Havergal, 1793-1870*

On Christmas Night All Christians Sing

192

1 On Christ - mas night all Chris - tians sing To
2 When sin de - parts be - fore⸺ Thy grace, Then
3 From out of dark - ness we⸺ have light, Which

hear the news⸺ the an - gels bring, On Christ - mas night all
life and health⸺ come in its place, When sin de - parts be -
made the an - gels sing this night, From out of dark - ness

Chris - tians sing To hear the news⸺ the an - gels bring,
fore⸺ Thy grace, Then life and health⸺ come in its place;
we⸺ have light, Which made the an - gels sing this night:

News of great joy,⸺ news of⸺ great mirth,
An - gels and men⸺ with joy⸺ may sing,
"Glo - ry to God⸺ and peace⸺ to men

News of our mer - ci - ful⸺ King's birth.
All for to see the new - born King.
Now and for - ev - er - more.⸺ A - men."

Text: English carol
Tune: **Sussex Carol**, *traditional carol*

193

On Eagle's Wings

And God will raise you up on ea - gle's wings,

bear you on the breath of dawn, make you to shine like the

sun, and hold you in the palm of God's hand.

Onward, Christian Soldiers 194

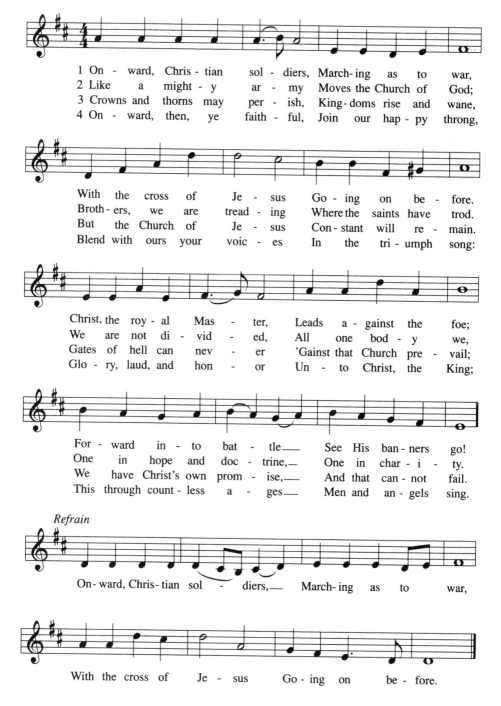

1 On - ward, Chris - tian sol - diers, March- ing as to war,
2 Like a might - y ar - my Moves the Church of God;
3 Crowns and thorns may per - ish, King- doms rise and wane,
4 On - ward, then, ye faith - ful, Join our hap - py throng,

With the cross of Je - sus Go - ing on be - fore.
Broth - ers, we are tread - ing Where the saints have trod.
But the Church of Je - sus Con - stant will re - main.
Blend with ours your voic - es In the tri - umph song:

Christ, the roy - al Mas - ter, Leads a - gainst the foe;
We are not di - vid - ed, All one bod - y we,
Gates of hell can nev - er 'Gainst that Church pre - vail;
Glo - ry, laud, and hon - or Un - to Christ, the King;

For - ward in - to bat - tle—— See His ban - ners go!
One in hope and doc - trine,—— One in char - i - ty.
We have Christ's own prom - ise,—— And that can - not fail.
This through count - less a - ges—— Men and an - gels sing.

Refrain

On- ward, Chris- tian sol - diers,—— March- ing as to war,

With the cross of Je - sus Go - ing on be - fore.

Text: Sabine Baring-Gould, 1834-1924
*Tune: **St. Gertrude**, Arthur S. Sullivan, 1824-1900*

195

Open Our Eyes

Pass It On

1 It___ on - ly takes a spark to get a fire___
2 What a won - drous time is spring when all the trees are
3 I___ wish for you, my friend, this hap - pi- ness that

go - ing, And soon all those a -
bud - ding, The birds be - gin to
I've found, You can de-pend on

round can warm up in its glow - ing.
sing, the flow - ers start their bloom - ing,
Him, it mat - ters not where you're bound.

That's how it is with God's___ love once you've ex-
That's how it is with God's___ love once you've ex-
I'll shout it from the moun-tain - top I want my

pe - ri-enced it; You spread His love to ev - 'ry- one; You
pe - ri-enced it; You want to sing, it's fresh like spring, You
world___ to know; The Lord of love has come to me, I

want to pass it on.
want to pass it on.
want to pass it on.

© Text: Kurt Kaiser, b. 1934
© Tune: Kurt Kaiser, b. 1934

197 Praise and Thanksgiving

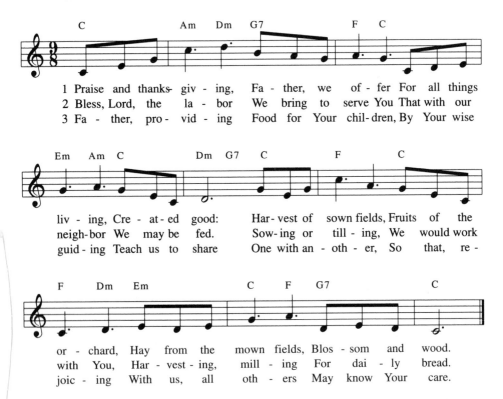

1 Praise and thanks- giv - ing, Fa - ther, we of - fer For all things
2 Bless, Lord, the la - bor We bring to serve You That with our
3 Fa - ther, pro - vid - ing Food for Your chil- dren, By Your wise

liv - ing, Cre - at - ed good: Har- vest of sown fields, Fruits of the
neigh- bor We may be fed. Sow- ing or till - ing, We would work
guid - ing Teach us to share One with an - oth - er, So that, re -

or - chard, Hay from the mown fields, Blos - som and wood.
with You, Har - vest - ing, mill - ing For dai - ly bread.
joic - ing With us, all oth - ers May know Your care.

© *Text: Albert F. Bayly, 1901-84, alt.*
Tune: **Bunessan**, *Gaelic*

Praise God, from Whom All Blessings Flow   198

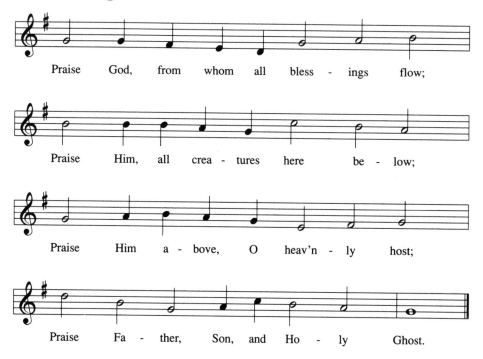

Praise God, from whom all bless - ings flow;

Praise Him, all crea - tures here be - low;

Praise Him a - bove, O heav'n - ly host;

Praise Fa - ther, Son, and Ho - ly Ghost.

Text: Thomas Ken, 1637-1711
*Tune: **Old Hundreth**, Louis Bourgeois, c. 1510-61*

199 Praise God. Praise Him

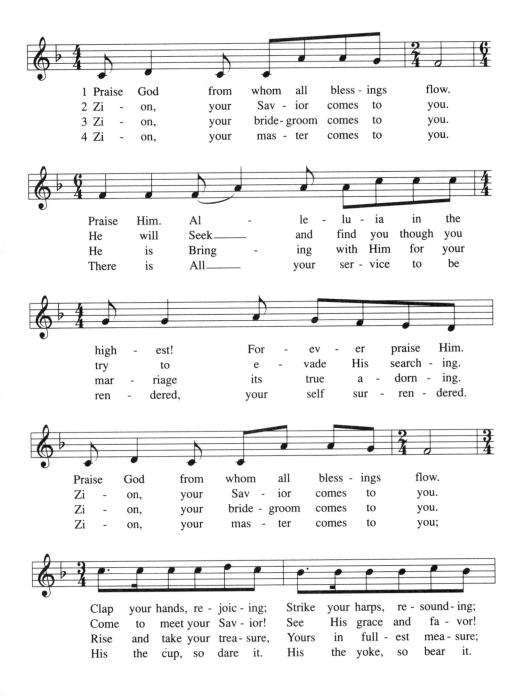

1 Praise God from whom all bless - ings flow.
2 Zi - on, your Sav - ior comes to you.
3 Zi - on, your bride- groom comes to you.
4 Zi - on, your mas - ter comes to you.

Praise Him. Al - le - lu - ia in the
He will Seek_____ and find you though you
He is Bring - ing with Him for your
There is All_____ your ser - vice to be

high - est! For - ev - er praise Him.
try to e - vade His search - ing.
mar - riage its true a - dorn - ing.
ren - dered, your self sur - ren - dered.

Praise God from whom all bless - ings flow.
Zi - on, your Sav - ior comes to you.
Zi - on, your bride - groom comes to you.
Zi - on, your mas - ter comes to you;

Clap your hands, re - joic - ing; Strike your harps, re - sound- ing;
Come to meet your Sav - ior! See His grace and fa - vor!
Rise and take your trea - sure, Yours in full - est mea - sure;
His the cup, so dare it. His the yoke, so bear it.

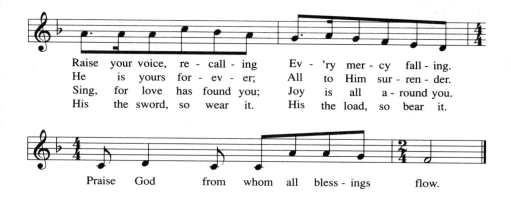

Raise your voice, re - call - ing   Ev - 'ry mer - cy fall - ing.
He   is   yours   for - ev - er;   All   to   Him   sur - ren - der.
Sing,   for   love   has   found you;   Joy   is   all   a - round you.
His   the   sword,   so   wear   it.   His   the   load,   so   bear   it.

Praise   God   from   whom   all   bless - ings   flow.

©Text: V. Masillamony Iyer, 20th cent.; tr. Daniel T. Niles, 1908-70, alt.
©Tune: **Tandanei,** Carnatic Tamil

200 Praise, My Soul, the King of Heaven

1 Praise, my soul, the King of heav - en;
2 Praise Him for His grace and fa - vor
3 Ten - der - ly He shields and spares us;
4 An - gels help us to a - dore Him,

To His feet your trib - ute bring.
To our fore - bears in dis - tress.
Well our fee - ble frame He knows.
Who be - hold Him face to face.

Ran - somed, healed, re - stored, for - giv - en,
Praise Him, still the same for - ev - er,
In His hands He gent - ly bears us,
Sun and moon bow down be - fore Him;

Ev - er - more His prais - es sing.
Slow to chide and swift to bless.
Res - cues us from all our foes.
All who dwell in time and space.

Al - le - lu - ia! Al - le - lu - ia!
Al - le - lu - ia! Al - le - lu - ia!
Al - le - lu - ia! Al - le - lu - ia!
Al - le - lu - ia! Al - le - lu - ia!

Praise the ev - er - last - ing King!
Glo - rious in His faith - ful - ness!
Wide - ly as His mer - cy flows.
Praise with us the God of grace.

Text: Henry F. Lyte, 1793-1847, alt.
*Tune: **Praise My Soul (Lauda anima)** John Goss, 1800-80*

Praise to the Lord, the Almighty 201

1 Praise to the Lord, the Al - might - y, the King of cre -
2 Praise to the Lord, who o'er all things is won - drous - ly
3 Praise to the Lord, who will pros - per your work and de -
4 Praise to the Lord! Oh, let all that is in me a -

a - tion! O my soul, praise Him, for
reign - ing And, as on wings of an
fend you; Sure - ly His good - ness and
dore Him! All that has life and breath,

He is your health and sal - va - tion!
ea - gle, up - lift - ing, sus - tain - ing.
mer - cy shall dai - ly at - tend you.
come now with prais - es be - fore Him!

Let all who hear Now to His tem - ple draw
Have you not seen All that is need - ful has
Pon - der a - new What the Al - might - y can
Let the a - men Sound from His peo - ple a -

near, Join - ing in glad ad - o - ra - tion!
been Sent by His gra - cious or - dain - ing?
do As with His love He be - friends you.
gain. Glad - ly for - ev - er a - dore Him!

Text: Joachim Neander, 1650-80; tr. Catherine Winkworth, 1829-78, alt.
*Tune: **Lobe den Herren**, Ernewertes Gesangbuch, Stralsund, 1665*

202 Promise Fulfilled

Capo 2

| (C) D | (Am) Bm | (Dm) Em | (G7) A7 |

1 "The King shall come,"   that was God's Word
2 The King has come,   our Sav - ior dear
3 The King now comes,   morn - ing has dawned
4 The King shall come,   let all a - wake

| (C) D | (Am) Bm | (Dm) Em | (G7) A7 |

Prom - ised of old,   to all who heard
The time ful - filled,   Je - sus is here!
Bright as the sun,   His light shines on
Pre - pare your hearts,   your lamps now take,

| (C) D | (Am) Bm | (Dm) Em | (G7) A7 |

The stump of Jes - se a righ - teous branch will grow
True God from all e - ter - ni - ty is born
Pierc - ing the shad - ows and dark - ness we have known
For like a bride-groom your Mas - ter soon draws near

| (C) D | (Am) Bm | (Dm) Em | (G7) A7 | (C) D |

Who will bring peace from the Fa - ther to His chil - dren here be - low.
God in the flesh now has come in - to the world on Christ-mas morn!
Fill - ing our lives with the joy and peace that He sends from the throne.
To wel-come home to the wed - ding feast the bride He loves so dear.

Rejoice in the Lord Always 203

Re - joice in the Lord__ al - ways and a-
gain I say re - joice. Re - joice in the Lord__
al - ways and a - gain I say re - joice. Re -
joice, re - joice, and a - gain I say re - joice. Re -
joice, re - joice, and a - gain I say re - joice.

204   Rejoice, O Pilgrim Throng

1 Re - joice, O pil - grim throng! Re-
2 With voice as full and strong As
3 With all the an - gel choirs, With
4 Yet on and on - ward still, With

joice, give thanks, and sing; Your fes - tal ban - ner
o - cean's surg - ing praise, Send forth the stur - dy
all the saints on earth Pour out the strains of
hymn and chant and song, Through gate and porch and

wave on high, The cross of Christ your king.
hymns of old, The psalms of an - cient days.
joy and bliss, True rap - ture, no - blest mirth.
col - umned aisle The hal - lowed path - ways throng.

Refrain

Re - joice! Re - joice! Re - joice, give thanks, and sing!

5 Still lift your standard high,
Still march in firm array,
As pilgrims through the darkness wend
Till dawns the golden day. *Refrain*

6 At last the march shall end;
The wearied ones shall rest;
The pilgrims find their home at last,
Jerusalem the blest. *Refrain*

7 Praise Him who reigns on high,
The Lord whom we adore:
The Father, Son, and Holy Ghost,
One God forevermore. *Refrain*

Text: *Edward H. Plumptre, 1821-91, alt.*
Tune: **Marion,** *Arthur H. Messiter, 1834-1916*

Savior of the Nations, Come 205

1 Sav - ior of the na - tions, come,
2 No man's pow'r of mind or blood
3 Here a maid was found with child,
4 Then stepped forth the Lord of all

Show Your - self the vir - gin's son.
But the Spir - it of our God
Vir - gin pure and un - de - filed.
From His pure and king - ly hall;

Mar - vel, heav - en, won - der, earth,
Made the Word of God be flesh,
In her vir - tues it was known
God of God, be - com - ing man,

That our God chose such a birth.
Wom - an's off - spring, pure and fresh.
God had made her heart His throne.
His he - ro - ic course be - gan.

5 God the Father was His source,
Back to God He ran His course.
Into hell His road went down,
Back then to His throne and crown.

6 Father's equal, You will win
Vict'ries for us over sin.
Might eternal, make us whole;
Heal our ills of flesh and soul.

7 From the manger newborn light
Sends a glory through the night.
Night cannot this light subdue,
Faith keeps springing ever new.

8 Glory to the Father sing,
Glory to the Son, our king,
Glory to the Spirit be
Now and through eternity.

©Text: attr. St. Ambrose, 340-97; German version Martin Luther, 1483-1546; tr. F. Samuel Janzow, b. 1913, alt.
Tune: **Nun komm, der Heiden Heiland,** Johann Walter, Geystliche gesangk Buchleyn, 1524

206

Savior, Stay with Me

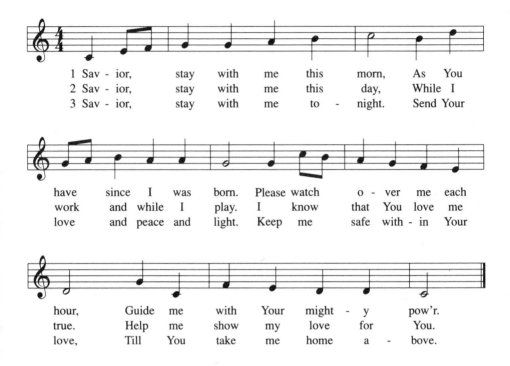

1 Sav - ior, stay with me this morn, As You
2 Sav - ior, stay with me this day, While I
3 Sav - ior, stay with me to - night. Send Your

have since I was born. Please watch o - ver me each
work and while I play. I know that You love me
love and peace and light. Keep me safe with - in Your

hour, Guide me with Your might - y pow'r.
true. Help me show my love for You.
love, Till You take me home a - bove.

©Text: Martin J. Maehr, 1984
Tune: **Gott sei Dank**, J. A. Freylinghausen, Geistreiches Gesang-Buch, 1704

Seek Ye First

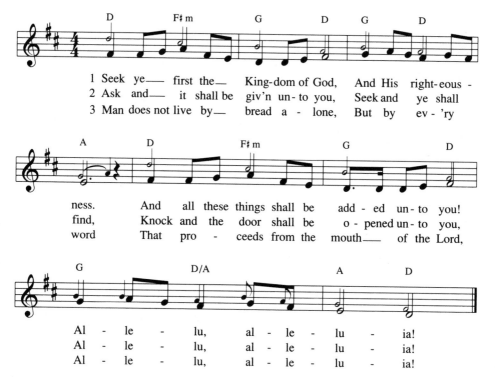

1 Seek ye___ first the___ King-dom of God, And His right-eous -
2 Ask and___ it shall be giv'n un- to you, Seek and ye shall
3 Man does not live by___ bread a - lone, But by ev - 'ry

ness. And all these things shall be add - ed un - to you!
find, Knock and the door shall be o - pened un- to you,
word That pro - ceeds from the mouth___ of the Lord,

Al - le - lu, al - le - lu - ia!
Al - le - lu, al - le - lu - ia!
Al - le - lu, al - le - lu - ia!

Text: Matthew 6:33
©*Tune: Karen Lafferty*

208 Sent Forth by God's Blessing

Sent forth by God's bless-ing, Our true faith con-fess-ing, The peo-ple of God from His dwell-ing take leave. The sup-per is end-ed. Oh, now be ex-tend-ed The fruits of this ser-vice in all who be-lieve. The seed of His teach-ing, Re-cep-tive souls reach-ing, Shall blos-som in ac-tion for God and for all. His grace did in-vite us, His love shall u-nite us To work for God's king-dom and an-swer His call.

© Text: Omer Westendorf, b. 1916, alt.
Tune: **The Ash Grove**, Welsh folk tune

Shalom, My Friends

Sha - lom, my friends! Sha - lom, my friends! Sha -

lom! Sha - lom! God's peace be with you! God's

peace be with you! Sha - lom! Sha - lom!

©Text: traditional Israeli canon; tr. Theodore Wuerffel, b. 1944, alt.
Tune: **Shalom, chaverim,** traditional Israeli canon

210 Shout for Joy, Loud and Long

1 Shout for joy, loud and long, God be praised
2 By God's word all was made, Heav'n and earth,
3 Yet our pride makes us fall! So Christ came
4 Now has Christ tru - ly ris'n And His spir -

with a song! To the Lord we be - long;
light and shade, Na - ture's won - ders dis - played,
for us all; Not the righ - teous to call;
it is giv'n To all those un - der heav'n

Chil - dren of our Mak - er, God the great life -
We to rule cre - a - tion From its first foun -
By His cross and pas - sion, Bring - ing us sal -
Who will walk be - side Him, Though they once de -

giv - er! Shout for joy, joy, joy!
da - tion. Shout for joy, joy, joy!
va - tion! Shout for joy, joy, joy!
nied Him! Shout for joy, joy, joy!

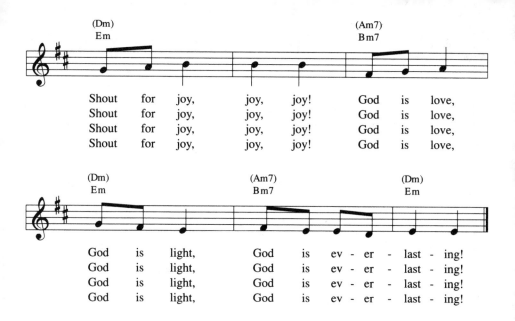

(Dm)					(Am7)		
Em					Bm7		

Shout for joy, joy, joy! God is love,
Shout for joy, joy, joy! God is love,
Shout for joy, joy, joy! God is love,
Shout for joy, joy, joy! God is love,

(Dm)			(Am7)			(Dm)	
Em			Bm7			Em	

God is light, God is ev - er - last - ing!
God is light, God is ev - er - last - ing!
God is light, God is ev - er - last - ing!
God is light, God is ev - er - last - ing!

©*Text: David Mowbray, b. 1938*
*Tune: **Personet hodie**, Piae contiones, 1582*

211 Silent Night! Holy Night

1 Si - lent night! Ho - ly night! All is calm,
2 Si - lent night! Ho - ly night! Shep - herds quake
3 Si - lent night! Ho - ly night! Son of God,

all is bright Round yon Vir - gin Moth - er and Child.
at the sight; Glo - ries stream— from heav - en a - far,
love's pure light Ra - diant beams— from Your ho - ly face

Ho - ly In - fant, so ten - der and mild, Sleep in heav - en - ly
Heav'n-ly hosts— sing, Al - le - lu - ia! Christ, the Sav - ior, is
With the dawn of re - deem - ing grace, Je - sus, Lord, at Your

peace,— Sleep— in heav - en - ly peace.
born!— Christ,— the Sav - ior, is born!
birth,— Je - sus, Lord, at Your birth.

Text: Joseph Mohr, 1792-1848; tr. John Freeman Young, 1820-85, alt.
*Tune: **Stille Nacht**, Franz Gruber, 1787-1863*

Silver and Gold

212

1 Sil - ver and gold have I none, But
2 Fear___ and hate have I none, Be -
3 Pow - er and strength have I none, But

such as I have give I thee; In the
cause___ of Je - sus Christ. He___
Je - sus gave___ me life So I

name of Je - sus Christ___ of
helped the blind___ to see___ So
cause___ He loves___ me so. Be -

Naz - a - reth, rise up and walk!
ev - 'ry - one stand up and praise.
cause___ He loves___ me so.

Refrain

He went walk - ing and leap - ing and prais - ing God,

walk-ing and leap-ing and prais-ing God. In the name of Je - sus

Christ___ of Naz - a - reth, rise up and walk.

Text: unknown
Tune: unknown

Sing a New Song to the Lord 213

1 Sing a new song to the Lord,
2 Now to the ends of the earth
3 Sing a new song and re - joice,
4 Join with the hills and the sea

He to whom won - ders be - long! Re -
See His sal - va - tion is shown; And
Pub - lish His prais - es a - broad! Let
Thun - ders of praise to pro - long! In

joice____ in His tri - umph and
still____ He re - mem - bers His
voic - es in cho - rus, with
judg - ment and jus - tice He

tell____ of His pow'r O
mer - cy and truth, Un -
trum - pet and horn, Re -
comes____ to the earth. O

sing to the Lord a new song!
chang - ing in love to His own.
sound for the joy of the Lord!
sing to the Lord a new song!

©Text: Timothy Dudley-Smith, b. 1926
©Tune: **Cantate Domino**, David G. Wilson, b. 1940

214

Sing, My Tongue

1 Sing, my tongue, the glo - rious bat - tle;
2 Tell how, when at length the full - ness
3 Thus, with thir - ty years ac - com - plished,
4 Faith - ful cross, true sign of tri - umph,

Sing the end - ing of the fray.
Of the ap - point - ed time was come,
He went forth from Naz - a - reth,
Be for all the no - blest tree;

Now a - bove the cross, the tro - phy,
He, the Word, was born of wom - an,
Des - tined, ded - i - cat - ed, will - ing,
None in fo - liage, none in blos - som,

Sound the loud tri - um - phant lay;
Left for us His Fa - ther's home,
Did His work, and met His death;
None in fruit Your e - qual be;

Tell how Christ, the world's re - deem - er,
Blazed the path of true o - be - dience,
Like a lamb He hum - bly yield - ed
Sym - bol of the world's re - demp - tion,

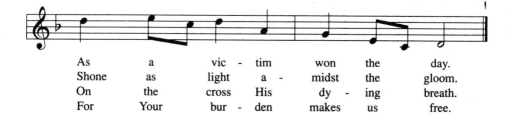

As	a	vic - tim	won	the	day.
Shone	as	light a -	midst	the	gloom.
On	the	cross His	dy - ing	breath.
For	Your	bur - den	makes	us	free.

5 Unto God be praise and glory;
To the Father and the Son,
To the eternal Spirit honor
Now and evermore be done;
Praise and glory in the highest
While the timeless ages run.

Text: Venantius Honorius Fortunatus, 530-609; tr. John M. Neale, 1818-66, alt.
©Tune: **Fortunatus New,** Carl F. Schalk, b. 1929

215 Sing to the Lord of Harvest

1 Sing to the Lord of har - vest, Sing
2 God makes the clouds rain good - ness, The
3 Bring to this sa - cred al - tar The

songs of love and praise; With joy - ful hearts and
des - erts bloom and spring, The hills leap up in
gifts His good-ness gave, The gold - en sheaves of

voic - es Your al - le - lu - ias raise. By
glad - ness, The val - leys laugh and sing. God
har - vest, The souls Christ died to save. Your

Him the roll - ing sea - sons In fruit - ful or - der
fills them with His full - ness, All things with large in -
hearts lay down be - fore Him When at His feet you

move; Sing to the Lord of
crease; He crowns the year with
fall, And with your lives a -

har - vest A joy - ous song of love.
bless - ing, With plen - ty and with peace.
dore Him Who gave His life for all.

Text: John S. B. Monsell, 1811-75, alt.
*Tune: **Wie lieblich ist der Maien**, Johann Steurlein, 1546-1613*

Somebody's Knockin' at Your Door

216

Some-bod-y's knock-in' at your door; Some-bod-y's knock-in' at your door; O_____ sin-ner, why don't you an-swer? Some-bod-y's knock-in' at your door.

Solo *All*

1 Knocks like Je - sus, Some-bod-y's knock-in' at your door;
2 Can't you hear Him?
3 Je - sus calls you,
4 Can't you trust Him?

Solo *All*

Knocks like Je - sus, Some-bod-y's knock-in' at your door.
Can't you hear Him?
Je - sus calls you,
Can't you trust Him?

O_____ sin - ner, why don't you an - swer?

Some - bod - y's knock-in' at your door.

Text: Afro-American spiritual
Tune: **Somebody's Knockin'**, *Afro-American spiritual*

217　　　　Someone Special

1 Some - one　Spe - cial,　I　know who:　That Some-one,　my
2 Some - one　Spe - cial,　that You　are,　To　cre - ate　the
3 Some - one　Spe - cial,　who would give　His　own　Son　that
4 Some - one　Spe - cial,　who would send　His　good　Spir - it

God,　is　You!　Who could make　a　world like　this
Christ- mas　Star,　Her - ald - ing　the　Sav - ior's birth,
all　might live,　And　by　Him would　set　us　free
for　a　Friend,　Faith Cre - a - tor,　Light　and Guide,

And　a　heav - en　full　of　bliss,　Some - one　spe - cial
Bring-ing peace and　joy　to　earth.　Some - one　spe - cial
From　all　sin　and　mis - e - ry.　Some - one　spe - cial
Al - ways stand- ing　at　my　side.　Some - one　spe - cial

I　must be,　Since You made　it　all　for　me!
I　must be,　Since You made that　Star　for　me!
I　must be,　Since You gave Your　Son　for　me!
I　must be　Since You gave that　Gift　to　me!

5 Someone Special—God and man,
　You were there when I began,
　You'll be there when I depart,
　For You live within my heart.
　Someone special—now I see,
　That someone is really me.

©Text: Jaroslav J. Vajda, b. 1919
©Tune: **Someone Special**, Carl Schalk, b. 1929

Soon and Very Soon

218

1 Soon and ver - y soon
2 No more cry - ing there, we are going to see the King!
3 No more dy - ing there,

Soon and ver - y soon
No more cry-ing there we are going to see the King!
No more dy-ing there,

Soon and ver - y soon
No more cry-ing there, we are going to see the King! Ha- le-

lu - jah! Hal-le - lu - jah! We're going to see the King!

going to see the King!

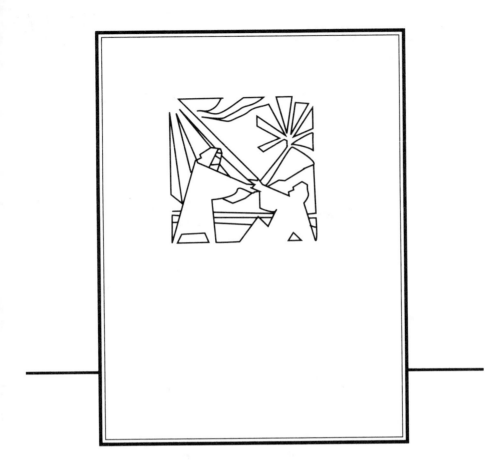

Soul's Celebration

219

Refrain

God is my strength, He is my sal - va-tion. God's strong right
hand has done might - y things. God is so great, my

Fine

soul's cel - e - bra-tion. God gives me words and makes my heart sing.

Cadence 1   Cadence 2   D.C.

Al- le-lu - ia, al - le - lu - ia,   Al-le-lu - ia, al - le-lu - ia,

Stanzas

1 E - vil sur - rounds me all my days; en - e - mies
2 Thanks to the Lord for He is good; His light shines

threat-en my life. God knows my needs and well pro -
bright-ly on me. This is the day the Lord has

Refrain

vides vic - to - ry con - quer- ing strife.   rit.
made. Be glad! Re - joice thank- ful - ly!

220 Standin' in the Need of Prayer

1 Not my broth - er, nor my sis - ter, but it's
2 Not the preach - er, nor the dea - con, but it's
3 Not my fa - ther, nor my moth - er, but it's
4 Not the stran - ger, nor my neigh - bor, but it's

me, O Lord, Stand - in' in the need of
me, O Lord, Stand - in' in the need of
me, O Lord, Stand - in' in the need of
me, O Lord, Stand - in' in the need of

prayer; Not my broth - er, nor my sis - ter, but it's
prayer; Not the preach - er, nor the dea - con, but it's
prayer; Not my fa - ther, nor my moth - er, but it's
prayer; Not the stran - ger, nor my neigh - bor, but it's

me, O Lord, Stand - in' in the need of prayer.
me, O Lord, Stand - in' in the need of prayer.
me, O Lord, Stand - in' in the need of prayer.
me, O Lord, Stand - in' in the need of prayer.

It's me,_____ it's me, O Lord,
It's me,

stand-in' in the need of prayer; It's me,_____ it's
It's me,

me, O Lord, Stand-in' in the need of prayer.

Text: Afro-American spiritual
Tune: Afro-American spiritual

221

Stay with Us

1 Stay with us, till night has come: our praise to
2 Walk with us, our spir-its sigh: hear when our
3 Walk with us, the road will bend: make all our
4 Talk with us, till we be-hold a joy-ful

You this day be sung. Bless our bread, o-pen our
wear-y spir-its cry Feel a-gain our loss, our
weep-ing, wail-ing end. Wipe our tears, for-give our
life You will un - fold: Heal our eyes to see the

eyes: Je-sus, be our great sur-prise.
pain: Je-sus, take us to your side.
fears: Je-sus, lift the heav - y cross.
prize: Je-sus, take us to the light.

5 Stay with us, till day is done: no tears nor dark shall dim the sun:
   Cheer the heart Your grace impart.
   Jesus, bring eternal life.

©Text: Herbert F. Brokering, b. 1926
©Tune: Walter L. Pelz, b. 1926

Sweetest Song
of This Bright Season
(*Dulces cantos entonemos*)

1 Sweet - est song of this bright sea - son Is the one glad
2 Hear the ho - ly an - gels sing - ing "Glo - ry be to
3 To that ho - ly Child be giv - ing All our lives though

hearts com - pose: Je - sus is the joy and rea - son
God on high!" To the world their song is bring - ing
weak and small, Then with Je - sus in us liv - ing,

For the peace His birth be - stows; So, all chil - dren
Joy and peace that will not die. So, all chil - dren
Tell and show His love to all: So, all chil - dren

sing and say: Peace and joy! It's Christ - mas Day!
sing and say: Peace and joy! It's Christ - mas Day!
sing and say: Peace and joy! It's Christ - mas Day!

1 Dulces cantos entonemos
A Jesús que Dios envió.
Bendición y paz tendremos
Al brindarle el corazón.
¡Niños todos entonad:
¡Gozo y paz! ¡Es Navidad!

2 Santos ángeles cantaron
Esa noche: «¡Gloria a Dios!»
Jubilosos proclamaron
Que nació el Salvador.
¡Niños todos entonad:
¡Gozo y paz! ¡Es Navidad!

3 Nuestras vidas consagremos
Al Niñito que nació.
Fieles todos proclamemos
La noticia del amor.
¡Niños todos entonad:
¡Gozo y paz! ¡Es Navidad!

223 Take My Life, O Lord, Renew

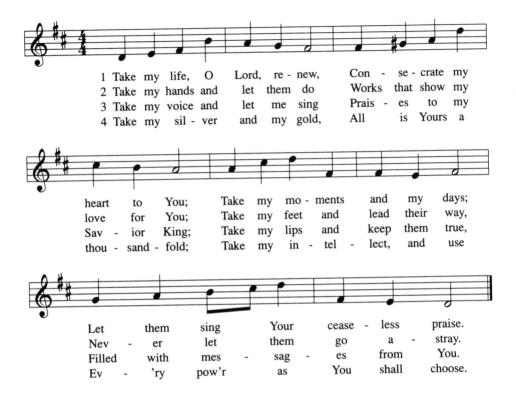

1 Take my life, O Lord, re - new,
   Con - se - crate my
2 Take my hands and let them do
   Works that show my
3 Take my voice and let me sing
   Prais - es to my
4 Take my sil - ver and my gold,
   All is Yours a

heart to You; Take my mo - ments and my days;
love for You; Take my feet and lead their way,
Sav - ior King; Take my lips and keep them true,
thou - sand - fold; Take my in - tel - lect, and use

Let them sing Your cease - less praise.
Nev - er let them go a - stray.
Filled with mes - sag - es from You.
Ev - 'ry pow'r as You shall choose.

5 Make my will Your holy shrine,
  It shall be no longer mine.
  Take my heart, it is Your own;
  It shall be Your royal throne.

6 Take my love; my Lord, I pour
  At Your feet its treasure store;
  Take my self, Lord, let me be
  Yours alone eternally.

Text: Frances R. Havergal, 1836-79, alt.
*Tune: **Patmos**, William H. Havergal, 1793-1870*

The Church's One Foundation 224

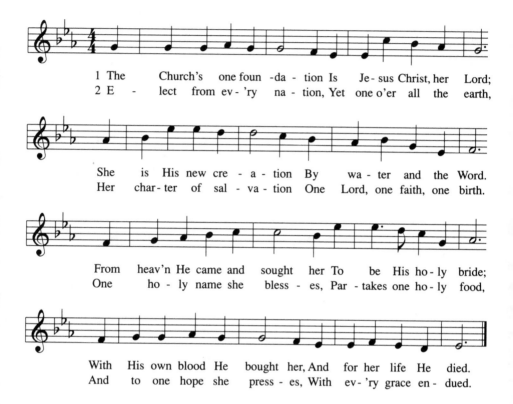

1 The Church's one foun-da-tion Is Je-sus Christ, her Lord;
2 E - lect from ev-'ry na-tion, Yet one o'er all the earth,

She is His new cre - a - tion By wa - ter and the Word.
Her char-ter of sal-va-tion One Lord, one faith, one birth.

From heav'n He came and sought her To be His ho-ly bride;
One ho-ly name she bless-es, Par-takes one ho-ly food,

With His own blood He bought her, And for her life He died.
And to one hope she press-es, With ev-'ry grace en-dued.

Text: Samuel J. Stone, 1839-1900
*Tune: **Aurelia,** Samuel S. Wesley, 1810-76*

The Fruit of the Spirit

The Head That Once Was Crowned

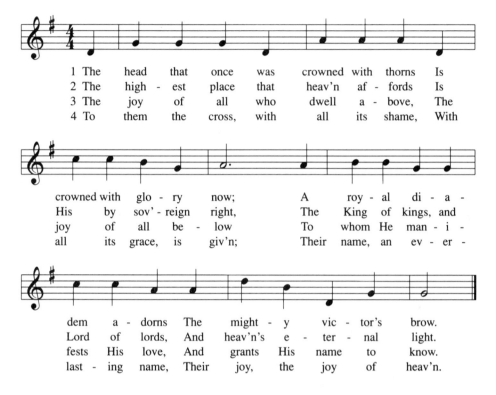

1 The head that once was crowned with thorns Is
2 The high - est place that heav'n af - fords Is
3 The joy of all who dwell a - bove, The
4 To them the cross, with all its shame, With

crowned with glo - ry now; A roy - al di - a -
His by sov' - reign right, The King of kings, and
joy of all be - low To whom He man - i -
all its grace, is giv'n; Their name, an ev - er -

dem a - dorns The might - y vic - tor's brow.
Lord of lords, And heav'n's e - ter - nal light.
fests His love, And grants His name to know.
last - ing name, Their joy, the joy of heav'n.

5 They suffer with their Lord below;
They reign with Him above,
Their profit and their joy to know
The myst'ry of His love.

6 The cross He bore is life and health,
Though shame and death to Him;
His people's hope, His people's wealth,
Their everlasting theme!

Text: Thomas Kelly, 1769-1854
*Tune: **Christ Triumphant,** John A. Behnke*

227 The King of Glory

Refrain

The King of Glo-ry comes, the na-tion re-joic-es;

O-pen the gates be-fore Him, lift up your voic-es.

1 Who is the King of Glo-ry; how shall we call Him?
2 In all of Gal-i-lee, in cit-y or vil-lage,
3 Sing then of Da-vid's son, our Sav-ior and Broth-er;
4 He gave His life for us, the Lamb of sal-va-tion,

He is Em-man-u-el, the Prom-ised of a-ges.
He goes a-mong His peo-ple cur-ing their ill-ness.
In all of Gal-i-lee was nev-er an-oth-er.
He took up-on Him-self the sins of the na-tion.

5 He conquered sin and death, He truly has risen,
And He will share with us His heavenly vision. *Refrain*

©*Text: Willard F. Jabusch, b. 1930*
*Tune: **The King of Glory**, Israeli folk song*

The King Shall Come

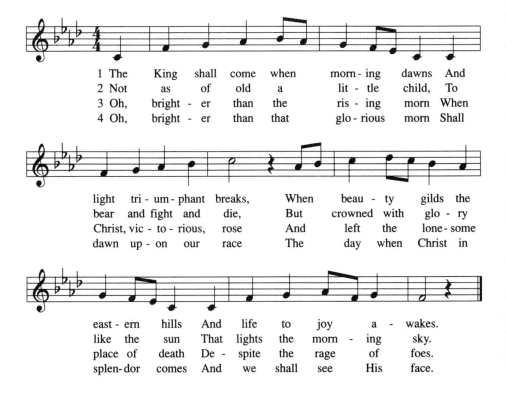

1 The King shall come when morn-ing dawns And
2 Not as of old a lit-tle child, To
3 Oh, bright-er than the ris-ing morn When
4 Oh, bright-er than that glo-rious morn Shall

light tri-um-phant breaks, When beau-ty gilds the
bear and fight and die, But crowned with glo-ry
Christ, vic-to-rious, rose And left the lone-some
dawn up-on our race The day when Christ in

east-ern hills And life to joy a-wakes.
like the sun That lights the morn-ing sky.
place of death De-spite the rage of foes.
splen-dor comes And we shall see His face.

5 The King shall come when morning dawns
And light and beauty brings.
Hail, Christ the Lord! Your people pray:
Come quickly, Kings of kings.

Text: John Brownlie, 1859-1925, alt.
*Tune: **Consolation,** John Wyeth, Repository of Sacred Music, Part II, 1813*

229 The Lamb

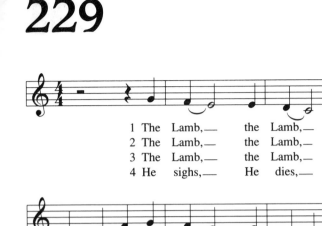

1 The Lamb,— the Lamb,— O Fa-ther, where's the
2 The Lamb,— the Lamb,— One per-fect fi - nal
3 The Lamb,— the Lamb,— As way-ward sheep their
4 He sighs,— He dies,— He takes my sin and

sac - ri - fice? Faith sees,— be - lieves— God will pro - vide the
of - fer-ing. The Lamb,— the Lamb,— Let earth join heaven His
shep - herd kill. So still,— His will— on our be - half the
wretch-ed- ness. He lives,— for - gives,— He gives me His own

Refrain

Lamb of price!
praise to sing.
Law to fill. Wor-thy is the Lamb whose death makes me His
righ-teous - ness.

own! The Lamb— is reign - ing on His throne!

5 He rose, He rose, My heart with thanks now overflows.
His song prolong 'Till ev'ry heart to Him belong. *Refrain*

The Law of God Is Good and Wise

1 The Law of God is good and wise
   And sets His will before our eyes,
   Shows us the way of righteousness,
   And dooms to death when we transgress.

2 Its light of holiness imparts
   The knowledge of our sinful hearts
   That we may see our lost estate
   And seek escape before too late.

3 To those who help in Christ have found
   And would in works of love abound
   It shows what deeds are His delight
   And should be done as good and right.

4 When men the offered help disdain
   And wilfully in sin remain,
   Its terror in their ear resounds
   And keeps their wickedness in bounds.

5 The Law is good; but since the fall
   Its holiness condemns us all;
   It dooms us for our sin to die
   And has no pow'r to justify.

6 To Jesus we for refuge flee,
   Who from the curse has set us free,
   And humbly worship at His throne,
   Saved by His grace through faith alone.

Text: Matthias Loy, 1828-1915
*Tune: **Erhalt uns Herr**, J. Klug, Geistliche Lieder, 1543*

231 The Lord Is My Light

1 The Lord is my Light and my Sal - va - tion;
2 I ask of the Lord for on - ly one thing,
3 Come hear me, O Lord, When - e'er I call You,
4 O Lord, will You teach me what to do here?

whom shall I fear? The Lord is the Strong - hold of my life.
this will I seek: to live in the Lord's house all my life.
an - swer me, Lord. I come to You now, I seek Your face.
Make my way safe; do not give me up, but lead me, Lord.

For He will hide me, and He will guide me;
In times of trou - ble He will pro - tect me,
Since You have helped me in all my tri - als,
I know You'll hide me and You will guide me.

He will set me high up - on a rock. The
He will keep me safe from ev - 'ry foe. I
Do not leave me now, O Lord, my Life. Come
Then have trust in God; do not de - spair. O

Lord is my Light and my Sal - va - tion;
ask of the Lord for on - ly one thing,
hear me, O Lord. When - e'er I call You,
Lord, will You teach me what to do here?

whom shall I fear? The Lord is the Strong - hold of my life.
this will I seek: to live in the Lord's house all my life.
an - swer me, Lord! I come to You now, I seek Your face.
Make my way safe; do not give me up, but lead me, Lord!

232

The Lord Is Present in His Sanctuary

1 The Lord is pres-ent in His sanc-tu-ar-y,
2 The Lord is pres-ent in His sanc-tu-ar-y,
3 The Lord is pres-ent in His sanc-tu-ar-y,

let us praise the Lord. The Lord is pres-ent in His
let us de-light in the Lord. The Lord is pres-ent in His
let us serve the Lord. The Lord is pres-ent in His

sanc-tu-ar-y, let us praise the Lord.
sanc-tu-ar-y, let us de-light in the Lord.
sanc-tu-ar-y, let us serve the Lord.

Praise Him, praise Him, let us praise the Lord.

Praise Him, praise Him, let us praise Je-sus.

The Lord's My Shepherd, I'll Not Want

233

1 The Lord's my shep - herd, I'll__ not want; He
2 My soul He doth re - store__ a - gain And
3 Yea, though I walk in death's__ dark vale, Yet
4 My ta - ble Thou hast fur - nish - ed In

makes__ me down__ to lie__ In pas - tures green; He
me__ to walk__ doth make__ With - in the paths of
will__ I fear__ no ill;__ For Thou art with me,
pres - ence of__ my foes;__ My head Thou dost with

lead - eth me The qui - et wa - ters by.
righ - teous - ness, E'en for__ His own name's sake.
and__ Thy rod And staff__ me com - fort still.
oil__ a - noint, And my__ cup o - ver - flows.

5 Goodness and mercy all my life
 Shall surely follow me;
 And in God's house forevermore
 My dwelling place shall be.

Text: The Psalms of David in Meeter, *Edinburgh, 1650*
Tune: **Belmont,** *William Gardiner, 1770-1853*

234

The Strife Is O'er, the Battle Done

Al - le - lu - ia, al - le - lu - ia, al - le - lu - ia!

1 The strife is o'er, the bat - tle done; Now is the
2 The pow'rs of death have done— their worst, But Christ their
3 The three sad days have quick - ly sped, He ris - es
4 He broke the age - bound chains— of hell; The bars from

vic - tor's tri - umph won; Now be the
le - gions has— dis - persed. Let shouts of
glo - rious from— the dead. All glo - ry
heav'n's high por - tals fell. Let hymns of

song of praise— be - gun. Al - le - lu - ia!
ho - ly joy— out - burst. Al - le - lu - ia!
to our ris - en head! Al - le - lu - ia!
praise His tri - umph tell. Al - le - lu - ia!

Al - le - lu - ia, al - le - lu - ia, al - le - lu - ia!

5 Lord, by the stripes which wounded You
From death's sting free Your servants too
That we may live and sing to You.
Alleluia!

Text: Symphonia Sirenum, Köln, 1695; tr. Francis Pott, 1832-1909, alt.
*Tune: **Victory**, Giovanni P. da Palestrina, 1525-94*

There Is a Green Hill Far Away 235

1 There is a green hill far a - way, Out -
2 We may not know, we can - not tell What
3 He died that we might be for - giv'n, He
4 There was no oth - er good e - nough To

side a cit - y wall, Where the dear Lord was
pains He had to bear, But we be - lieve it
died to make us good, That we might go at
pay the price of sin, He on - ly could un -

cru - ci - fied, Who died to save us all.
was for us He hung and suf - fered there.
last to heav'n, Saved by His pre - cious blood.
lock the gate Of heav'n and let us in.

5 Oh, dearly, dearly has He loved!
And we must love Him too
And trust in His redeeming blood
And try His works to do.

Text: Cecil Francis Alexander, 1818-95, alt.
*Tune: **Horsley**, William Horsley, 1774-1858*

236

There Is a Name
I Love to Hear

1 There is a name I love to hear;
2 It tells me of a Sav - ior's
3 It tells me what my Fa - ther
4 It tells of One whose lov - ing

hear; I love to sing its worth.
love, Who died to set me free.
hath In store for ev - 'ry day
heart Can feel my deep - est woe,

It sounds like mu - sic in my
It tells me of His pre - cious
And though I tread a dark - some
Who in each sor - row bears a

ear, The sweet - est name on earth.
blood, The sin - ner's per - fect plea.
path, Yields sun - shine all the way.
part That none can bear be - low.

Refrain

Oh, how I love Je - sus,

Oh, how I love Je - sus!

Oh, how I love Je -

sus, be - cause___ He first loved me!

Text: Frederick Whitfield, 1829-1904
Tune: **Oh, How I Love Jesus,** *American melody, 19th cent.*

237 They'll Know We Are Christians by Our Love

Capo 1   E♭m / Fm

1 We are one in the Spir - it, We are
2 We will walk with each oth - er, We will
3 We will work with each oth - er, We will
4 All__ praise to the Fa - ther, From__

A♭m / B♭m

one in the Lord, We are one in the
walk hand in hand, We will walk with each
work side by side, We will work with each
whom all things come, And all praise to Christ

E♭m / Fm

Spir - it, We are one in the Lord, And we
oth - er, We will walk hand in hand, And to -
oth - er, We will work side by side, And we'll
Je - sus, His__ on - ly__ Son, And all

A♭m / B♭m   E♭m / Fm

pray that all u - ni - ty may one day be re -
geth - er we'll spread the news that God is in our
guard each man's dig - ni - ty and save each man's
praise to the Spir - it, who__ makes__ us__

C / D♭

stored. And they'll know we are Chris - tians by our
land.
pride.
one.

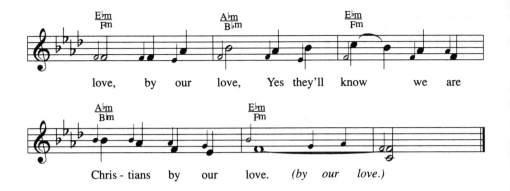

love,   by   our   love,   Yes they'll   know   we   are

Chris - tians   by   our   love.   *(by   our   love.)*

238 This Is a Joyous, Happy Day

This is a joy-ous, hap-py day; We cel-e-brate Your gift of life. Christ is with us, joy sur-rounds us. Christ takes our sin and sets us free; He fills our lives with end-less life. Christ is with us; Christ u-nites us. Praise our Mak-er, praise the Spir-it, Praise Christ Je - sus.

This Is He

239

1 In a low-ly man-ger born, Hum-ble life be-
2 Vis-it-ing the lone and lost, Stead-y-ing the
3 Then, to res-cue you and me, Je-sus died up-

gun in scorn; Un-der Jo-seph's watch-ful eye,
tem-pest-tossed, Giv-ing of Him-self in love,
on the tree. See in Him God's love re-vealed;

Je-sus grew as you and I; Knew the suf-f'rings
Call-ing minds to things a-bove. Sin-ners glad-ly
By His pas-sion we are healed. Now He lives in

of the weak, Knew the pa-tience of the meek,—
hear His call; Pub-li-can be-fore Him fall,—
glo-ry bright Lives a-gain in pow'r and might;—

Hun-gered as but poor folk can;
For in Him new life be-gan;
Come and take the path He trod,

This is He. Be-hold the man!
This is He. Be-hold the man!
Son of Mar-y, Son of God.

©Text: Koh Yuki, b. 1923
©Tune: **Woodridge,** Richard W. Gieseke, b. 1952

240 This Is My Commandment

This is my com-mand-ment that you love one an-oth-er, that your

joy may be full full: that your

joy may be full, that your

joy may be full.

Other stanzas may be added: This is my commandment that you trust one another . . . .
serve one another . . . .
lay down your lives . . . .

Text: John 15:11-12
Tune: unknown

This Is the Day

This is the day, this is the day that the Lord hath made, that the Lord hath made. I will re-joice, I will re-joice and be glad in it, and be glad in it, This is the day that the Lord hath made, we will re-joice and be glad in it. This is the day, this is the day that the Lord hath made.

242   This Is the Feast of Victory

C This is the feast_____ of vic-to-ry for our God. Al-le-lu-ia, al-le-lu-ia, al-le-lu-ia!

I Wor-thy is Christ, the Lamb who was slain, whose blood set us free_____ to be peo-ple of God.

C This is the feast_____ of vic-to-ry for our God. Al-le-lu-ia, al-le-lu-ia, al-le-lu-ia.

II Pow-er, rich-es, wis-dom, and strength, and hon-or,_____ bless-ing, and glo-ry are His.

C This is the feast_____ of vic-to-ry for our God. Al-le-lu-ia, al-le-lu-ia, al-le-lu-ia.

I Sing with all the peo-ple of God, and join in the hymn of all cre-a - tion: Bless-ing, hon-or, glo-ry, and might be to God and the Lamb for-ev-er. A - men.

C This is the feast of vic-to-ry for our God. Al-le-lu - ia, al-le - lu-ia, al-le-lu - ia.

II For the Lamb who was slain has be-gun His reign. Al-le-lu - ia.

C This is the feast of vic-to-ry for our God. Al-le-lu - ia, al-le-lu-ia, al-le-lu - ia!

243   This Joyful Eastertide

1 This joy - ful Eas - ter - tide, A -
2 Death's flood has lost its chill Since
3 My flesh in hope shall rest And

way with sin and sor - row! My
Je - sus crossed the riv - er; Lov -
for a sea - son slum - ber Till

Love, the Cru - ci - fied, Has sprung to life this mor -
er of souls, from ill My pass - ing soul de - liv -
trump from east to west Shall wake the dead in num -

Refrain

row Had Christ, who once was slain, not burst His
er:
ber:

three - day pris - on, Our faith had been in vain But

now has Christ a - ris - en, a - ris - en, a - ris - en; But

now has Christ a - ris - en!

©*Text: George R. Woodward, 1848-1934*
Tune: **Vruechten,** *Dutch tune, 17th cent.*

Those Who Trust in the Lord 244

1 Those who trust in the Lord are like Mount Zi - on, which can
2 Wrong will not al-ways rule o'er God's own peo-ple, for God's
3 Through the qui-et of time God watch - es o'er us, God a -

nev - er be shak - en, nev-er be moved. As the moun-tains sur-
love is the pow - er God is the Lord. Lord, be good to all
bove and be-neath us, here yet be-yond. We can trust in His

round Je - ru - sa - lem, so the Lord sur-rounds His peo-ple from
peo - ple born to earth; may Your heal - ing love up - hold us, u -
full and con-stant love, for the Lord sur-rounds His peo-ple from

now on and for - ev - er.
nit - ing and re - stor - ing.
now on and for - ev - er.

©Text: Heinz Werner Zimmermann, b. 1930, st. 1; Marjorie Jillson, b. 1931, sts. 2-3
©Tune: Heinz Werner Zimmermann, b. 1930

245

Thy Loving-Kindness

1 Thy lov-ing-kind-ness is bet-ter than
2 I lift my hands up un-to the
3 I lift my voice up un-to the
4 I lift my heart up un-to the

1 Thy lov-ing-kind-ness is bet-ter than
2 I lift my hands up un-to the
3 I lift my voice up un-to the
4 I lift my heart up un-to the

is bet-ter than life. Thy lov-ing-
un-to the Lord. I lift my
un-to the Lord. I lift my
un-to the Lord. I lift my

life Thy lov-ing-kind-ness
Lord. I lift my hands up
Lord. I lift my voice up
Lord. I lift my heart up

246   Thy Strong Word

1 Thy strong word did cleave the darkness;
2 Give us lips to sing Thy glory,

At Thy speaking it was done;
Tongues Thy mercy to proclaim,

For created light we thank Thee,
Throats that shout the hope that fills us,

While Thine ordered seasons run.
Mouths to speak Thy holy name.

Al - le - lu - ia, al - le - lu - ia!
Al - le - lu - ia, al - le - lu - ia!

Praise to Thee who light dost send!
May the light which Thou dost send

Al - le - lu - ia, al - le - lu - ia!
Fill our songs with al - le - lu - ias,

Al - le - lu - ia with - out end!
Al - le - lu - ias with - out end!

©Text: Martin H. Franzmann, 1907-1976
©Tune: **Ebenezer**, Thomas John Williams, 1869-1944

Thy Word Is a Lamp

Thy word is a lamp un-to my feet and a
light un-to my path.

2 Now

1 When I feel a-fraid,____ think I've lost my way,
I will not for-get Your love for me and yet my

still You're there right be - side me, and
heart for - ev - er is wan - der - ing.

noth - ing will I fear as long as You are near.
Je - sus, be my guide and hold me to Your side, and

Please be near me to the end.____
I will love You to the end.____

©Text: Amy Grant
©Tune: **Thy Word**, Michael W. Smith

248 To Him Who by the Pow'r

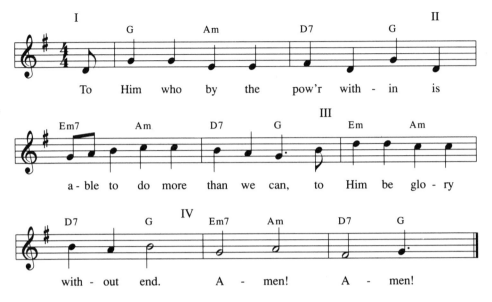

To Him who by the pow'r with - in is
a - ble to do more than we can, to Him be glo - ry
with - out end. A - men! A - men!

Today Your Mercy Calls Us 249

1 To - day Your mer - cy calls us To wash a - way our sin.
2 To - day Your gate is o - pen, And all who en - ter in
3 To - day our Fa - ther calls us, His Ho - ly Spir - it waits;

How - ev - er great our tres - pass, What - ev - er we have been,
Shall find a Fa - ther's wel - come And par - don for their sin.
His bless - ed an - gels gath - er A - round the heav'n - ly gates.

How - ev - er long from mer - cy Our hearts have turned a - way,
The past shall be for - got - ten, A pres - ent joy be giv'n,
No ques - tion will be asked us How of - ten we have come;

Your pre - cious blood can wash us And make us clean to - day.
A fu - ture grace be prom - ised, A glo - rious crown in heav'n.
Al - though we oft have wan - dered, It is our Fa - ther's home.

Text: Oswald Alle, 1816-78, alt.
*Tune: **Anthes,** J. A. Anthes, 1789-1842*

250

Wake Us, O Lord, to Human Need

1 Wake us, O Lord, to hu - man need To go wher - ev - er You would lead. A - wake our sens - es so that we More sen - si - tive to needs may be.

2 Un - blind our eyes so we may see The masks that cov - er mis - er - y, The hid - den tear, the wor - ried frown, The lone - li - ness of those let down.

3 Lord, free our hands for heal - ing touch To reach to those who've suf - fered much: Re - tard - ed child, de - lin - quent, poor; Your love, a - live in us, the cure.

4 Since you've re - deemed us from de - spair, You've freed us so that we can share; Our neigh - bors' prob - lems now we'll bear. Be - cause You love, we love and care!

©Text: Phyllis Kersten, b. 1939
Tune: **Tallis' Canon**, Thomas Tallis, c. 1510-85

We Are Climbing Jacob's Ladder

251

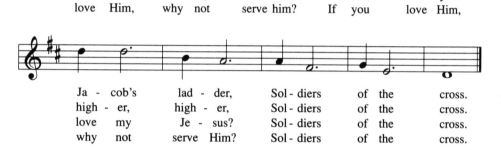

1 We are climb-ing Ja-cob's lad-der, We are
2 Ev-'ry round goes high-er, high-er, Ev-'ry
3 Sin-ner, do you love my Je-sus? Sin-ner,
4 If you love Him. why not serve Him? If you

climb-ing Ja-cob's lad-der. We are climb-ing
round goes high-er, high-er, Ev-'ry round goes
do you love my Je-sus? Sin-ner, do you
love Him, why not serve him? If you love Him,

Ja-cob's lad-der, Sol-diers of the cross.
high-er, high-er, Sol-diers of the cross.
love my Je-sus? Sol-diers of the cross.
why not serve Him? Sol-diers of the cross.

5 We are climbing higher, higher,
We are climbing higher, higher,
We are climbing higher, higher,
Soldiers of the cross.

Text: Afro-American spiritual
Tune: Afro-American spiritual

252

We Are the Church

Refrain

I am the church! You are the church!

We are the church to - geth - er!

All who fol - low Je - sus All a - round the world!

Yes, we're the church to - geth - er!

1 The church is not a build - ing, The
2 We're man - y kinds of peo - ple, With
3 And when the peo - ple gath - er There's
4 At Pen - te - cost some peo - ple Re -

church is not a stee - ple, The
man - y kinds of fac - es, All
sing - ing and there's pray - ing, There's
ceived the Ho - ly Spir - it And

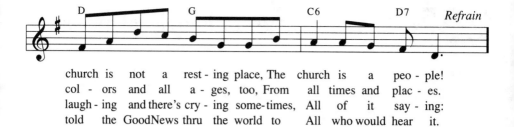

church is   not   a   rest - ing place, The   church is   a   peo - ple!
col - ors   and   all   a - ges, too, From   all   times and   plac - es.
laugh - ing   and there's cry - ing some-times, All   of   it   say - ing:
told   the GoodNews thru   the world to   All   who would hear   it.

5 I count if I am ninety Or nine or just a baby;
  There's one thing I am sure about and I don't mean maybe; *Refrain*

©*Text: Richard Avery, b. 1934; Donald Marsh, b. 1923*
©*Tune: Richard Avery, b. 1934; Donald Marsh, b. 1923*

253   We Come, O Lord, This Day

1 We come, O Lord, this day, we
2 We come, O Lord, this day, we
3 We come, O Lord, this day, we

lift our hearts to pray;   We bring our songs of
bow our heads to pray;   En - a - ble us to
bow our heads to pray;   For - give us when we

grate - ful praise, our psalms of joy to
do Your will, make clear our goals and
fail to do an act of love that

You we raise, we wor - ship You in ev - 'ry way.
guide us still, that we may serve You day by day.
pleas - es You, for - give us when we turn a - way.

We Come to Praise You

1 Heav - en - ly Fa - ther, we come to praise You, And to say
2 Je - sus, our Sav - ior, we love and fol - low, For all the
3 Com - fort - ing Spir - it, move us to wor - ship, Show-ing Christ's

thank You here in our song, For all the gifts You give through Your
bless- ings You died to share; Life and sal - va - tion we have for -
love in all that we do. Help us to serve our broth - ers and

kind - ness, Show - ing Your love, for - giv - ing our wrong.
ev - er, Trust - ing Your mer - cy, know - ing Your care.
sis - ters, Know - ing the off'r - ing's giv - en to You.

Tune: **Bunessan,** Gaelic

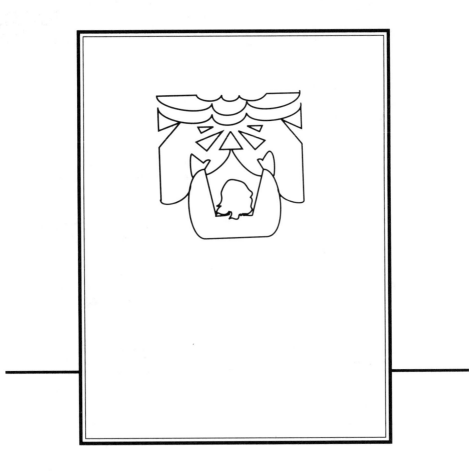

We Give You But Your Own   255

1 We give You but Your own In
2 May we Your boun - ties thus As
3 Hearts still are bruised and dead, And
4 To com - fort and to bless, To

an - y gifts we bring; All that we have is
stew - ards true re - ceive And glad - ly, Lord, as
homes are bare and cold, And lambs for whom the
find a balm for woe, To tend those lost in

Yours a - lone, A trust from You, our King.
You bless us, To You our first - fruits give.
Shep - herd bled Are stray - ing from the fold.
lone - li - ness Is an - gels' work be - low.

5 The captive to release,
   The lost to God to bring,
   To teach the way of life and peace,
   It is a Christ-like thing.

6 And we believe Your word,
   Though dim our faith, it's true:
   What we do for Your people, Lord,
   We do it all for You.

Text: William W. How, 1823-97, alt.
*Tune: **Energy**, William H. Monk, 1823-89*

256

We Praise Thee, O God

We praise—— Thee, O God; we ac - knowl- edge Thee to

be the Lord. All the earth doth wor - ship Thee the

Fa - ther ev - er - last - ing.

To Thee all an - gels cry a - loud, the

heav'ns and all the powers there - in.—————— To Thee

cher - u - bim and ser - a - phim con - tin - ual - ly do

cry: Ho - ly, ho - ly,

ho - ly, Lord God of Sab - a - oth;

and on - ly Son; al - so the

Ho - ly Ghost, the Com - fort - er.

Thou art the

King of Glo - ry, O___ Christ. Thou art the

ev - er - last - ing Son of the Fa - ther.

Day by___ day we mag-ni - fy___ Thee; and we

wor - ship Thy name___ ev - er, world with - out end.

We Praise You, O God

257

1 We praise You, O God, our Re-deem-er, Cre-a-tor;
2 We wor-ship You, God of our fa-thers, we bless You;
3 With voic-es u-nit-ed our prais-es we of-fer

In grate-ful de-vo-tion our trib-ute we bring.
Through tri-al and tem-pest our guide You have been.
And glad-ly our songs of thanks-giv-ing we raise.

We lay it be-fore You, we kneel and a-dore You;
When per-ils o'er-take us, You will not for-sake us,
With You, Lord, be-side us, Your strong arm will guide us.

We bless Your ho-ly name,— glad prais-es we sing.
And with Your help, O Lord,— our strug-gles we win.
To You, our great Re-deem-er, for-ev-er be praise!

Text: Julia C. Cory, 1882-1963, alt.
*Tune: **Kremser**, Nederlandtsch Gedenckclanck, Haarlem, 1626*

258   We Shall Not Be Moved: Psalm 1

1 How bless-ed are the ones who nev-er walk With-
2 Our joy is in the stat-utes of the Lord, And
3 The wick-ed shall not stand the judg-ment day, But
4 Sing glo-ry be to God, the Fa-ther, Son, And

in the place where wick-ed scof-fers talk.
night and day we pon-der on the Word.
like the chaff they'll all be blown a-way. We're like a
Ho-ly Spir-it, ev-er Three in One.

tree that's plant-ed by the wa-ter. We shall not be moved!

We shall not, we shall not be moved! We shall not,

we shall not be moved! We're like a tree that's plant-ed by the

wa-ter. We shall not be moved!

We Shall Overcome

259

1 We shall o - ver - come,____ We shall o - ver - come,____
2 We'll walk hand in hand,____ We'll walk hand in hand,____
3 We shall all have peace,____ We shall all have peace,____
4 We are not a - fraid,____ We are not a - fraid,____
5 God is on our side,____ God is on our side,____

We shall o - ver - come some - day.____ Oh,____
We'll walk hand in hand some - day____ Oh,____
We shall all have peace some - day.____ Oh,____
We are not a - fraid this day.____ Oh,____
God is on our side this day.____ Oh,____

If in our hearts we do be - lieve,
If in our hearts we do be - lieve,
If in our hearts we do be - lieve,
If in our hearts we do be - lieve,
If in our hearts we do be - lieve,

We shall o - ver - come some - day.
We'll walk hand in hand some - day.
We shall all have peace some - day.
We are not a - fraid this day.
God is on our side this day

260

We Thank You, Lord, for Eyes to See

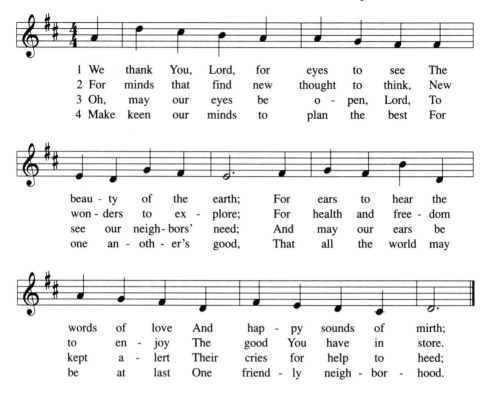

1 We thank You, Lord, for eyes to see The
2 For minds that find new thought to think, New
3 Oh, may our eyes be o - pen, Lord, To
4 Make keen our minds to plan the best For

beau - ty of the earth; For ears to hear the
won - ders to ex - plore; For health and free - dom
see our neigh - bors' need; And may our ears be
one an - oth - er's good, That all the world may

words of love And hap - py sounds of mirth;
to en - joy The good You have in store.
kept a - lert Their cries for help to heed;
be at last One friend - ly neigh - bor - hood.

©Text: *Jeanette E. Perkins*
Tune: **Ellacombe,** Gesangbuch der Herzogl. Hofkapelle, *Württemberg, 1784*

What a Friend We Have in Jesus

261

1 What a friend we have in Je-sus, All our sins and griefs to bear!
2 Have we tri-als and temp-ta-tions? Is there trou-ble an-y-where?
3 Are we weak and heav-y-lad-en, Cum-bered with a load of care?

What a priv-i-lege to car-ry Ev-'ry-thing to God in prayer!
We should nev-er be dis-cour-aged— Take it to the Lord in prayer.
Pre-cious Sav-ior, still our ref-uge— Take it to the Lord in prayer.

Oh, what peace we of-ten for-feit; Oh, what need-less pain we bear—
Can we find a friend so faith-ful Who will all our sor-rows share?
Do your friends de-spise, for-sake you? Take it to the Lord in prayer.

All be-cause we do not car-ry Ev-'ry-thing to God in prayer!
Je-sus knows our ev-'ry weak-ness— Take it to the Lord in prayer.
In His arms He'll take and shield you; You will find a sol-ace there.

Text: Joseph Scriven, 1820-86
*Tune: **Converse,** Charles Crozat Converse, 1832-1918*

262

What Child Is This

1 What child is this, who, laid to rest, On
2 Why lies He in such mean es - tate Where
3 So bring Him in - cense, gold, and myrrh, Come

Mar - y's lap is sleep - ing? Whom an - gels greet with
ox and ass are feed - ing? Good Chris - tian, fear; for
peas - ant, king, to own Him. The King of kings sal -

an - thems sweet While shep - herds watch are keep - ing?
sin - ners here The si - lent Word is plead - ing.
va - tion brings; Let lov - ing hearts en - throne Him.

This, this is Christ the King, Whom shep - herds guard and
Nails, spear shall pierce Him through, The cross be borne for
Raise, raise the song on high, The Vir - gin sings her

an - gels sing: Haste, haste to bring Him laud, The
me, for you; Hail, hail the Word made flesh, The
lu - la - by; Joy, joy, for Christ is born, The

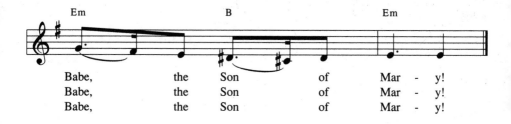

	Babe,	the	Son	of	Mar	-	y!
	Babe,	the	Son	of	Mar	-	y!
	Babe,	the	Son	of	Mar	-	y!

Text: William Chatterton Dix, 1837-98
Tune: **Greensleeves,** *English ballad, 16th cent.*

263

What God Ordains Is Always Best

1 What God or - dains is al - ways good: His
2 What God or - dains is al - ways good: He
3 What God or - dains is al - ways good: This

will is just and ho - ly. As He di - rects my
is my friend and fa - ther; He suf - fers naught to
truth re - mains un - shak - en. Though sor - row, need, or

life for me, I fol - low meek and low - ly. My
do me harm, Though man - y storms may gath - er. Now
death be mine, I shall not be for - sak - en. I

God in - deed In ev - 'ry need Knows
I may know Both joy and woe, Some -
fear no harm, For with His arm He

well how He will shield me; To Him, then, I will yield me.
day I shall see clear - ly That He has loved me dear - ly.
shall em - brace and shield me; So to my God I yield me.

Text: Samuel Rodigast, 1649-1708; tr. The Lutheran Hymnal, 1941, alt.
*Tune: **Was Gott tut**, Severus Gastorius, c. 1650-93*

Whatsoever You Do

Refrain

Whatsoever you do to the least of My broth - ers, That you do un - to Me.

1 When I was hun - gry, you gave Me to eat;
2 When I was wea - ry, you helped Me find rest;
3 Hurt in a bat - tle, you bound up My wounds;
4 When I was home - less, you o - pened your door;

When I was thirst - y, you gave Me to drink.
When I was anx - ious, you calmed all My fears.
Search - ing for kind - ness, you held out your hand.
When I was na - ked, you gave Me your coat.

Now en - ter in - to the home of My Fa - ther.

5 When I was little, you taught Me to read;
  When I was lonely, you gave Me your love. *Refrain*

6 When in a prison, you came to My cell;
  When on a sick bed, you cared for My needs. *Refrain*

©Text: Willard F. Jabusch, b. 1930
©Tune: **Whatsoever You Do,** Willard F. Jabusch, b. 1930

265 When Christ's Appearing Was Made Known

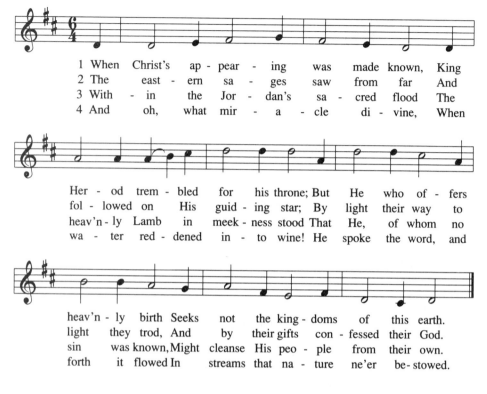

1 When Christ's ap-pear-ing was made known, King
2 The east-ern sa-ges saw from far And
3 With-in the Jor-dan's sa-cred flood The
4 And oh, what mir-a-cle di-vine, When

Her-od trem-bled for his throne; But He who of-fers
fol-lowed on His guid-ing star; By light their way to
heav'n-ly Lamb in meek-ness stood That He, of whom no
wa-ter red-dened in-to wine! He spoke the word, and

heav'n-ly birth Seeks not the king-doms of this earth.
light they trod, And by their gifts con-fessed their God.
sin was known, Might cleanse His peo-ple from their own.
forth it flowed In streams that na-ture ne'er be-stowed.

5 For this His glad epiphany
All glory unto Jesus be,
Whom with the Father we adore,
And Holy Ghost forevermore.

Text: Coelius Sedulius, 5th cent.; tr. composite
*Tune: **Puer nobis nascitur**, adapt. Michael Praetorius, 1571-1621*

When I Survey the Wondrous Cross

1 When I sur - vey the___ won - drous___ cross
2 For - bid it, Lord, that___ I should___ boast
3 See, from His head, His___ hands, His___ feet
4 Were the whole realm of___ na - ture___ mine,

On which the prince of___ glo - ry___ died,
Save in the death of___ Christ, my___ God;
Sor - row and love flow___ min - gled___ down.
That were a trib - ute___ far too___ small;

My rich - est gain I___ count but___ loss
All the vain things that___ charm me___ most,
Did e'er such love and___ sor - row___ meet
Love so a - maz - ing,___ so di - vine,

And pour con - tempt on all my___ pride.
I sac - ri - fice them to His___ blood.
Or thorns com - pose so rich a___ crown?
De - mands my soul, my life, my___ all.

Text: Isaac Watts, 1674-1748
*Tune: **Hamburg**, Lowell Mason, 1792-1872*

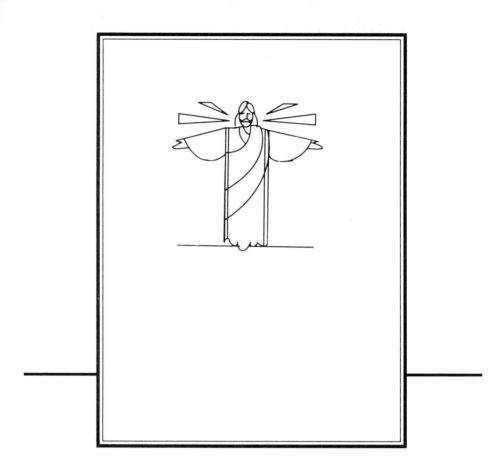

When in Our Music God Is Glorified

1 When in our mu - sic God is glo - ri -
2 How oft, in mak - ing mu - sic, we have
3 So has the Church, in lit - ur - gy and
4 And did not Je - sus sing a psalm that

fied And ad - o - ra - tion leaves no room for pride, It
found A new di - men - sion in the world of sound As
song, In faith and love, through cen - tu - ries of wrong, Borne
night When ut - most e - vil strove a - gainst the light? Then

is as though the whole cre - a - tion cried:___
wor - ship moved us to a more pro - found___
wit - ness to the truth in ev - 'ry tongue:___
let us sing, for whom He won the fight:___

Al - le-lu - ia, al - le-lu - ia, al - le-lu - ia!

5 Let ev'ry instrument be tuned for praise;
Let all rejoice who have a voice to raise;
And may God give us faith to sing always:
Alleluia, alleluia, alleluia!

©*Text: F. Pratt Green, b. 1903*
©*Tune: **Fredericktown,** Charles R. Anders, b. 1929*

268

Who Was the Man

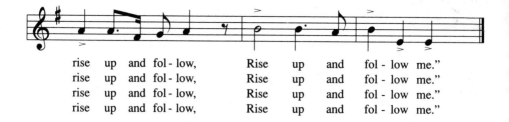

rise   up   and fol - low,   Rise   up   and   fol - low me."
rise   up   and fol - low,   Rise   up   and   fol - low me."
rise   up   and fol - low,   Rise   up   and   fol - low me."
rise   up   and fol - low,   Rise   up   and   fol - low me."

Yes

Refrain

And God said Yes to you! He said Yes to me When the

Bap-tism wa-ter flowed free-ly. In the name of the Fa - ther, the

Spir - it, the Son, Our jour - ney of faith had be -

1. gun. And God said

2. gun.

1 Oh, it's a -
2 But there's the
3 Oh, each and

maz-ing grace in - deed That would save some-one like me: Saved by
dev - il on the prowl Seek - ing whom he may de- vour Off'r- ing
ev - 'ry day is great It's a day to cel - e - brate What the

grace so a - maz - ing - ly free. Oh, it's an
all kinds of for - tune and fame. But when the
Lord, in His mer - cy, has done. What - ev - er

awe-some, love - ly sound, It's the sweet-est sound a - round; It's the
dev - il seeks his due For the things he's of - fered you, Just say,
an - y day shall bring Live each day for Christ the King! Live each

Refrain

Good News for you and for me. That God said
"No! I don't play Sa - tan's game!" And God said
day as a vic - to - ry won! And God said

270

You Are My Own

1 The splash of the wa - ter! The pow'r of the
2 To Him you be - long now: His grace be a -
3 Your faith is a gra - cious Mir - a - cu - lous

Word!— The Spir - it now binds you to Je - sus your
dored!— His grace which sus - tains as you grow in the
gift:— A mir - a - cle just like His ris - ing from

Lord! And won - der of won - ders! Though by sin de -
Word! And grace of all grac - es! The vic - t'ry He
death. Both mir - a - cles yours now In Bap - tis - m's

filed,— The Fa - ther in heav - en Now makes you His child!
won— Is your vic - t'ry now through your faith in the Son!
flood— Se - cured by the cov - e - nant sealed with His blood.

A child of the prom - ise His death has ful -

filled! An heir of the cov - e - nant sure as His

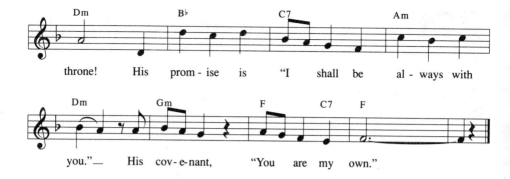

throne! His prom - ise is "I shall be al - ways with

you."— His cov - e - nant, "You are my own."

You Have Put on Christ

You have put on Christ, In Him you have been bap- tized.

Al - le - lu - ia, al - le - lu - ia.

©Text: International Committee on English in the Liturgy, 1969
©Tune: Howard Hughes, b. 1930

ACKNOWLEDGMENTS

The liturgical material on pages 7–27 is covered by the copyright of this book.

The catechism translation is copyright ©1986 Concordia Publishing House.

The prayers on pages 28–34 are covered by the copyright of this book.

Every effort has been made to determine copyright holders of the texts, tunes, and settings included in this book. The publisher regrets any errors or oversights which may have occurred and will readily make proper acknowledgement in future editions if such omissions are made known. The following copyright holders are gratefully acknowledged:

50 **Setting:** From *A Heritage of Hymns.* Copyright © 1972 Concordia Publishing House.

51 **Text:** From *Lutheran Book of Worship,* copyright © 1978. By permission of Concordia Publishing House.

52 **Text:** "A Christmas Hymn" from ADVICE TO A PROPHET AND OTHER POEMS, copyright 1961 and renewed 1989 by Richard Wilbur, reprinted by permission of Harcourt Brace Jovanovich, Inc.
Tune and Setting: Copyright ©1984 by GIA Publications, Inc., Chicago, IL. All rights reserved. Used by permission.

53 **Text:** Copyright ©1985 Board for Youth Services, The Lutheran Church—Missouri Synod. Used with permission.

55 **Setting:** From *The Parish Organist.* Copyright ©1953 Concordia Publishing House.

56 **Setting:** From *A Heritage of Hymns.* Copyright ©1972 Concordia Publishing House.

58 **Text:** Copyright ©1961, 1989 by John W. Peterson Music Company. All rights reserved. Used by permission.

59 **Tune and setting:** Copyright ©1972, by MANNA MUSIC, INC., 25510 Ave. Stanford, Suite 101, Valencia, CA 91355. International Copyright Secured. All Rights Reserved. Used by Permission.

60 **Setting:** From *A Heritage of Hymns.* Copyright ©1972 Concordia Publishing House.

61 **Setting:** From a choral octavo (98-2350) by Carl Schalk, copyright ©1978 Concordia Publishing House.

62 **Setting:** From *The Parish Organist.* Copyright ©1953 Concordia Publishing House.

64 **Text, tune, and setting:** Copyright ©1985 John Ylvisaker. Used by permission.

111 **Text:** Copyright ©1983, Jaroslav J. Vajda. All rights reserved. Used by permission.
Tune and Setting: Copyright ©1983 by GIA Publications, Inc., Chicago, IL. All rights reserved.
112 **Text:** Copyright ©1958. Renewal 1986 by Hope Publishing Co., Carol Stream, IL 60188. All rights reserved. Used by permission.
Setting: From *Worship Supplement.* Copyright ©1969 Concordia Publishing House.
113 **Text:** From *Lutheran Book of Worship,* copyright ©1978. By permission of Concordia Publishing House.
Tune and setting: From the *English Hymnal* by permission of Oxford University Press. Simplified by permission of Oxford University Press.
115 **Text, tune and setting:** Copyright ©1973 Concordia Publishing House.
116 **Text:** Copyright © Concordia Publishing House.
Setting: From *The International Book of Christmas Carols,* ©1963. By permission of Walter Ehret.
118 **Setting:** Copyright ©1978 by Lillenas Publishing Co. All rights reserved. Used by permission.
121 **Text and tune:** Copyright ©1967 by Hope Publishing Co., Carol Stream, IL 60188. All rights reserved. Used by permission.
122 **Text, tune, and setting:** Copyright ©1981 and this arrangement ©1992 Meadowgreen Music Co. International Copyright Secured. All Rights Reserved. Used By Permission.
124 **Setting:** Copyright ©1983 by Song Productions, Minneapolis MN. All Rights Reserved.
125 **Setting:** Copyright ©1982 Concordia Publishing House.
126 **Setting:** From *The Parish Organist.* Copyright ©1963 Concordia Publishing House.
128 **Text:** (Additional verses) Copyright ©1991 Jeffrey E. Burkart. Used by permission.
129 **Text, tune, and setting:** Copyright ©1978 HOUSE OF MERCY MUSIC (Administered by MARANATHA! MUSIC, c/o THE COPYRIGHT COMPANY, NASHVILLE, TN) All Rights Reserved. International Copyright Secured. Used By Permission.
131 **Text:** Words by Lesbia Scott; used by permission of Morehouse Publishing, P.O. Box 1321, Harrisburg, PA 17105.
Tune and setting: Copyright ©1965 Graded Press. Used by permission.
132 **Setting:** Copyright ©1955 Concordia Publishing House.
133 **Setting:** Copyright ©1977 by Lillenas Publishing Co. All rights reserved. Used by permission.
134 **Setting:** Copyright ©1977 Richmond Music.
135 **Tune and setting:** Copyright Harry T. Burleigh. Used by permission.
136 **Text:** From "A New Hymnic Setting of Divine Service III" (98-2989). Copyright ©1991 Concordia Publishing House.
Setting: From *Worship Supplement.* Copyright ©1969 Concordia Publishing House.

137 **Setting:** From *Worship Supplement.* Copyright ©1969 Concordia Publishing House.

138 **Text:** Copyright ©1960 Evans Bros. Ltd. Used by permission. **Setting:** From *Lutheran Book of Worship,* copyright ©1978. By permission of Concordia Publishing House.

141 **Text, tune, and setting:** Copyright ©1969 by Hope Publishing Co., Carol Stream, IL 60188. All rights reserved. Used by permission.

142 **Setting:** From *A Heritage of Hymns.* Copyright ©1972 Concordia Publishing House.

145 **Text, tune, and setting:** Copyright ©1974 *Scripture in Song.* All Rights Reserved. International Copyright Secured. Administered By MARANATHA! MUSIC C/O THE COPYRIGHT COMPANY, NASHVILLE, TN) Used By Permission.

146 **Tune and setting:** Copyright ©1981 Les Presses de Taizé (France). Used by permission of GIA Publications, Inc. Chicago, IL, exclusive agent. All rights reserved. Used by permission.

149 **Tune and setting:** © Copyright, 1965, World Library Publications, Inc. All rights reserved. Used with permission.

150 **Text, tune, and setting:** Copyright ©1976 Birdwing Music/Cherry Lane Music Publishing Co., Inc. All rights controlled and adminstered by the Sparrow Corp., PO Box 5010, Brentwood, TN 37024-5010. All rights reserved. International copyright secured. Used by permission of Sparrow Corporation.

151 **Text, tune, and setting:** Copyright ©1980 MARANATHA! MUSIC. (Administered By THE COPYRIGHT COMPANY, NASHVILLE, TN) All Rights Reserved. International Copyright Secured. Used By Permission.

152 **Text, tune, and setting:** Copyright ©1971 CELEBRATION (Administered by MARANATHA! MUSIC, c/o THE COPYRIGHT COMPANY, NASHVILLE, TN) All Rights Reserved. International Copyright Secured. Used by permission.

153 **Text:** International Consultation on English Texts. **Tune and setting:** From *Lutheran Book of Worship,* copyright ©1978. By permission of Concordia Publishing House.

154 **Setting:** From the *Worship Supplement.* Copyright ©1969 Concordia Publishing House.

155 **Text:** Copyright ©1939, renewed 1966, by E.C.Schirmer Music Company. Used by permission.

157 **Text:** From *Book of Common Prayer* The Episcopal Church 1979. Reprinted by permission. **Tune and setting:** From *Lutheran Book of Worship,* copyright ©1978. By Permission of Concordia Publishing House.

158 **Setting:** *Lutheran Book of Worship,* copyright ©1978. By permission of Concordia Publishing House.

159 **Setting:** From *The Parish Organist.* Copyright ©1953 Concordia Publishing House.

160 **Text, tune, and setting:** Copyright ©1983 by Terry K. Dittmer. Used with permission.

161 **Text and tune:** Copyright ©1921 by Edward B. Marks Company. Copyright Renewed. International Copyright Secured. All Rights Reserved. Used by Permission.

162 **Text, tune, and setting:** Copyright ©1974 by Hope Publishing Co., Carol Stream, IL 60188. All rights reserved. Used by permission.

163 **Text, tune, and setting:** Copyright ©1976 by Hinshaw Music, Inc. Reprinted by permission.

164 **Text, tune, and setting:** From *Contemporary Worship 5.* Copyright ©1972 by the Inter-Lutheran Commission on Worship, Concordia Publishing House representing the copyright holders.

165 **Text, tune, and setting:** Copyright ©1978 Prism Tree Music. Administered by Bob Kilpatrick Music, P.O. Box 2383, Fair Oaks, CA 95628. All rights reserved. Used by permission.

167 **Text:** From *Enlarged Songs of Praise* by permission of Oxford University Press.

168 **Text:** Copyright © 1969 Concordia Publishing House.

169 **Setting:** From *A Heritage of Hymns.* Copyright ©1972 Concordia Publishing House.

170 **Text and tune:** ©1963 by Galliard Ltd. Used by permission of Galaxy Music Corp., Boston.

171 **Text:** From *Lutheran Book of Worship,* copyright ©1978. By permission of Concordia Publishing House.

172 **Text:** By permission of Oxford University Press. Stanza 3 slightly altered and stanza 4 omitted by permission of Oxford University Press.
Setting: From *Lutheran Book of Worship,* copyright ©1978. By permission of Concordia Publishing House.

173 **Text and tune:** Copyright ©1969 by Songs and Creations, Inc., P.O. Box 7, San Anselmo CA 94979. All rights reserved. Used by Permission.

174 **Text, tune, and setting:** Copyright ©1982 WILLING HEART MUSIC (Administered by MARANATHA! MUSIC c/o THE COPYRIGHT COMPANY, NASHVILLE, TN) All Rights Reserved. International Copyright Secured. Used by permission.

176 **Tune:** By permission of the Successor to Dr. John Ireland.
Setting: From *Worship Supplement.* Copyright ©1969 Concordia Publishing House.

177 **Text:** From *Lutheran Book of Worship.* Copyright ©1978. By permission of Concordia Publishing House.

178 **Text:** International Consultation on English Texts
Tune and setting: Copyright ©1982 Concordia Publishing House.

179 **Text, tune, and setting:** Copyright ©1971 by Communiqué Music, Inc., (ASCAP), administered by Copyright Management, Inc. International Copyright Secured. All Rights Reserved. Used by permission.

181 **Setting:** From *The Parish Organist.* Copyright ©1953 Concordia Publishing House.

183 **Tune and setting:** From the *English Hymnal.* By permission of Oxford University Press.

184 **Text:** From *¡Cantad al Senor!* Copyright ©1991 Concordia Publishing House.
Translation: Copyright ©1992 Concordia Publishing House
Setting: Copyright Leonido Krey. Used by permission.

186 **Setting:** From *Our Songs of Praise.* Copyright ©1954 Concordia Publishing House.

189 **Text:** Copyright © Gerhard Cartford. Used by permission.
Setting: From *¡Cantad al Senor!* Copyright ©1991 Concordia Publishing House.

190 **Setting:** From *The Parish Organist.* Copyright ©1953 Concordia Publishing House.

192 **Text and tune:** Copyright Stainer Bell Ltd. All rights reserved. Used by permission.

193 **Text, tune, and setting:** Copyright ©1979, New Dawn Music, P.O. Box 13248, Portland OR 97213. All rights reserved. Used with permission.

195 **Text, tune, and setting:** Copyright ©1976 MARANATHA! MUSIC (Administered by THE COPYRIGHT COMPANY, NASHVILLE, TN) All Rights Reserved. International Copyright Secured. Used by permission.

196 **Text, tune, and setting:** Copyright ©1969 by Communiqué Music, Inc., (ASCAP), administered by Copyright Management, Inc. International Copyright Secured. All Rights Reserved. Used by permission.

197 **Text:** By permission of Oxford University Press. Stanza 4 omitted with permission by Oxford University Press.
Setting: From *Carols for the Seasons.* Copyright ©1959 Concordia Publishing House.

198 **Setting:** From *The Parish Organist.* Copyright ©1963 Concordia Publishing House.

199 **Text:** Copyright Daniel T. Niles. Used by permission of the Christian Conference of Asia.
Tune: Copyright John Milton Kelley. Used by permission of the Christian Conference of Asia.

202 **Text and tune:** Copyright ©1989 James E. Fritsche. Used by permission.
Setting: Copyright ©1992 Concordia Publishing House.

203 **Text, tune, and setting:** Copyright ©1967 by Word Music (a div. of WORD, INC.). All Rights Reserved. International Copyright Secured. Used by permission.

205 **Setting:** From *Worship Supplement.* Copyright ©1969 Concordia Publishing House.

206 **Text:** Copyright ©1986 Concordia Publishing House.
Setting: Copyright ©1982 Concordia Publishing House.

207 **Text, tune, and setting:** Copyright ©1972 MARANATHA! MUSIC (Administered By THE COPYRIGHT COMPANY NASHVILLE, TN) All Rights Reserved. International Copyright Secured. Used by permission.

208 **Text:** Copyright ©1964 World Library Publications, Inc. All rights reserved. Used with permission.

209 **Text:** Translation from *Praise the Lord.* Copyright ©1973 Concordia Publishing House.

210 **Text:** Copyright ©1982 by Hope Publishing Co., Carol Stream, IL 60188. All rights reserved. Used by permission.
Setting: Copyright ©1984 GIA Publications, Inc., Chicago, IL. All rights reserved.

212 **Setting:** Copyright ©1992 Concordia Publishing House.

213 **Text, tune, and setting:** Copyright ©1973 by Hope Publishing Co., Carol Stream, IL 60188. All rights reserved. Used by permission.

Tune: Copyright © Richard Hillert. Used by permission.
Setting: Copyright ©1992 Richard Hillert. Used by permission.
243 **Text:** {Oxford} From the *Cowley Carol Book* by permission of A.R.Mowbray & Co., Ltd., Oxford England.
Setting: Copyright ©1969 Concordia Publishing House.
244 **Text, tune, and setting:** Copyright ©1973 Concordia Publishing House.
245 **Text and tune:** Copyright ©1956. Singspiration Music/ASCAP (chorus) and Copyright © 1962 by Singspiration/ASCAP (verses) All Rights Reserved. Used by permission of Benson Music Group, Inc.
246 **Text:** Copyright ©1969 Concordia Publishing House.
Tune: Copyright Gwenlyn Evans, Ltd. Used by permission.
Setting: From *Worship Supplement.* Copyright ©1969 Concordia Publishing House.
247 **Text, tune, and setting:** Copyright ©1984 and this arrangement ©1992 Meadowgreen Green Music Co./Bug & Bear Music. International Copyright Secured. All Rights Reserved. Used By Permission.
248 **Text and tune:** Copyright ©1976 John Ylvisaker. Used by permission.
Setting: Copyright ©1992 Concordia Publishing House.
249 **Setting:** From *The Parish Organist.* Copyright ©1963 Concordia Publishing House.
250 **Text:** Copyright Phyllis N. Kersten. Used by permission.
252 **Text, tune, and setting:** Copyright ©1972 by Hope Publishing Co., Carol Stream, IL 60188. All rights reserved. Used by permission.
253 **Text, tune, and setting:** Copyright ©1981 Choristers Guild. Used by permission.
254 **Text:** Copyright ©1990 Concordia Publishing House.
Setting: From *Carols for the Seasons.* Copyright ©1959 Concordia Publishing House.
255 **Setting:** Copyright ©1982 Concordia Publishing House.
256 **Text, tune, and setting:** Copyright ©1953 Concordia Publishing House.
258 **Text and tune:** Copyright ©1976 Concordia Publishing House.
259 **Text and tune:** Musical and Lyrical adaptation by Zilphia Horton, Frank Hamilton, Guy Carawan, and Pete Seeger. Inspired by African American Gospel Singing, members of the Food & Tobacco Workers Union, Charleston, SC, and the southern Civil Rights Movement. TRO—© Copyright 1960 (renewed 1988) and 1963 (renewed 1991) Ludlow Music, Inc., New York, NY. International Copyright Secured. Made In U.S.A. All Rights Reserved Including Public Performance For Profit. Royalties derived from this composition are being contributed to the We Shall Overcome Fund and The Freedom Movement under the Trusteeship of the writers.
Setting: Copyright ©1992 Concordia Publishing House.
260 **Text:** Copyright ©1964. Used by permission of The Pilgrim Press.
264 **Text and tune:** Copyright ©1966, 1985 by Willard F. Jabusch, 5735 S. University, Chicago IL 60637.
267 **Text:** Copyright ©1972 by Hope Publishing Co., Carol Stream, IL 60188. All rights reserved. Used by permission.

TOPICAL INDEX

285

291

Social Concern

Suffering/Comfort

Trinity

SCRIPTURAL INDEX

Genesis	1:3	Thy Strong Word 246
	2:7	Breath of the Living God 77
	5:24	Lord, Take My Hand and Lead Me 171
	6:9	Life Is a Journey 160
	22:1-19	The Lamb 229
	28:10-17	Alleluia to Jesus 61
		We Are Climbing Jacob's Ladder 251
Exodus	15:1-2	Earth and All Stars 90
	19:4	On Eagle's Wings 193
	19:9-13	Oh, Come, Oh, Come, Emmanuel 186
	23:19	We Give You But Your Own 255
	33:20	Holy, Holy, Holy 119
Deuteronomy	10:12	O God of Mercy, God of Light 182
	32:4	What God Ordains Is Always Good 263
Joshua	1:6	Sent Forth by God's Blessing 208
1 Samuel	2:1-11	My Soul Now Magnifies the Lord 177
		My Soul Proclaims the Greatness 178
2 Samuel	22:3	I Am Trusting You, Lord Jesus 126
1 Kings	8:35-36	Forgive Us, Lord, for Shallow Thankfulness 97
	8:66	Sent Forth by God's Blessing 208
1 Chronicles	16:23-36	Praise to the Lord, the Almighty 201
	16:31-36	Oh, That I Had a Thousand Voices 190
		When in Our Music God Is Glorified 267
Ezra	3:11	Praise to the Lord, the Almighty 201
Nehemiah	9:6	Praise to the Lord, the Almighty 201
Job	1:21	Children of the Heavenly Father 80
	19:25-27	King of Kings 151
	38:7	A Stable Lamp is Lighted 52

	6:10a	In You Is Gladness 137
	8:9	Oh, Come, All Ye Faithful 185
	13:14	Go, My Children, with My Blessing 102
		I've Got the Joy 140
Galatians	3:26-29	In Christ There Is No East or West 135
	3:27	You Have Put on Christ 271
	4:4-7	Dear Christians, One and All, Rejoice 88
	5:22-26	The Fruit of the Spirit 225
	6:2	A Time to Serve 53
		Wake Us, O Lord, to Human Need 250
	6:14	Sing, My Tongue 214
		When I Survey the Wondrous Cross 266
Ephesians	1:3-8	Blest the Children of Our God 75
		Christ, the Life of All the Living 82
	1:3-14	We Come to Praise You 254
	1:11	All Things Work Out for Good 58
	2:4-8	Amazing Grace! How Sweet the Sound 63
	2:8-10	You Are My Own 270
	2:11-22	Lord of All Nations, Grant Me Grace 168
	2:19-22	We Are the Church 252
	2:20	The Church's One Foundation 224
		We Praise You, O God 256
	2:20-22	What God Ordains Is Always Good 263
	3:5	We Praise You, O God 256
	3:11	All Things Work Out for Good 58
	3:12	My Faith Looks Trustingly 175
	3:20-21	To Him Who by the Pow'r 248
	4:4-6	The Church's One Foundation 224
		Onward, Christian Soldiers 194
	4:11	We Praise You, O God 256
	5:19-20	Praise and Thanksgiving 197
	6:18	Every Time I Feel the Spirit 93
	6:23	Go, My Children, with My Blessing 102
	6:24	Take My Life, O Lord, Renew 223
Philippians	2:5-11	Dear Christians, One and All, Rejoice 88
		Jesus, Name Above All Names 145
		Lord, I Want to Be a Christian 166
	2:9-11	There Is a Name I Love to Hear 236
	3:8	When I Survey the Wondrous Cross 266
	4:4	Rejoice in the Lord Always 203
		Rejoice, O Pilgrim Throng 204
	4:4-7	I've Got the Joy 140
Colossians	3:11-14	In Christ There Is No East or West 135

SONGS AND HYMNS IN CANON

* indicates where second voice begins.

TITLE AND
FIRST LINE INDEX

311